A New Setting of Ignatius' Spiritual Exercises:
Hearing, Seeing, Feeling Old Stories in New Ways

imagined by

Brian J. Shircliff &
the Companions of VITALITY Cincinnati
2015

Publication of this book has been underwritten by Peg & Joe Conway, in gratitude for the healing mission of VITALITY Cincinnati. We are grateful to you, Conway Family!

Cover image "Ignatius Portrait" by Holly Schapker
<u>Adsum</u>: Contemporary Paintings on Ignatian Spirituality (2010)
We are grateful to you, Holly!

This book has been published as a fundraiser for VITALITY Cincinnati. All proceeds from sales of this book benefit the mission of VITALITY Cincinnati: sharing holistic self-care from neighborhood to neighborhood, person to person, and breath by breath since 2010.

We are very grateful to four Cincinnatians for their contributions to this book: Holly Schapker, Walter Brueggemann, Nikki Giovanni, and Julie Lucas. Holly Schapker has shared her beautiful painting "Ignatius Portrait" for the cover of this book. "Ignatius Portrait" is part of *Adsum*: Contemporary Paintings on Ignatian Spirituality (2010) and can be found at www.hollyschapker.com. Dr. Walter Brueggemann, perhaps the greatest imaginer of the Hebrew Scriptures of our day, inspired the sections on lament that appear in the "Week Three" invitations. Dr. Brueggemann's Lenten lecture series at Episcopal Church of the Redeemer and around Greater Cincinnati in 2010 and 2011 have given many of us reason to imagine new ways of proceeding in our culture and our grief-filled lives around the world. World-renowned poet Nikki Giovanni, who grew up in Lincoln Heights (northern Cincinnati neighborhood), has given us her blessing to use a part of her life-story in this book. Julie Lucas (withinwonder.com) designed our beautifully inspiring VITALITY logo in 2010 and designed the map on this book's cover. May we be so bold as Holly, Walter, Nikki, and Julie in our imaginings!

Every effort has been made to give credit to other people's original ideas through the endnotes that follow this text. If you feel something should be credited to someone and is not, please get in touch through the website above and every effort will be made to correct this text for future printings. Thank you!

We invite you to honor your mind, your body, your whole self. Do only what you know to be right for you. While the invitations offered here in this book are geared to be gentle and easily modified by the reader to fit the reader's needs, please consult your medical doctor or health professional before undertaking any practices shared or alluded to within this book.

First published by Dog Ear Publishing
4011 Vincennes Rd
Indianapolis, IN 46268
www.dogearpublishing.net

ISBN: 978-1-4575-4153-7

This book is printed on acid-free paper.

Printed in the United States of America

CONTENTS

Inspiration & Dedication

It was at the tomb of Pedro Arrupe, S.J., that a vision for this new setting of the Spiritual Exercises was conceived during a quick visit in Rome. I had about two hours free until I needed to catch a train to meet with my colleagues in Assisi. We were rendezvousing in Assisi for a few days before we hunkered down on Francis of Assisi's mountain, La Verna, to write and ponder and converse about Ignatius Loyola's Spiritual Exercises.

So I stopped into the Gesu, adult-home to Ignatius Loyola after he founded the Jesuits with his companions. The Church of the Gesu where Ignatius died in the simple apartment next door sits about a mile from the Colosseum. My feet were badly blistered from so much walking and exploring Ignatius' old haunts in Spain the previous ten days: Montserrat, Manresa, Barcelona. As many know, Ignatius conceived much of the Spiritual Exercises while recuperating from war-wounds in Spain. It is said that he began writing these Exercises in his recovery bed in Loyola then during his own pilgrimage to Montserrat and eventually the year-plus stay in Manresa. Being in these places that were so pivotal in Ignatius' life was profound, for sure, but something in me was restless there.

My feet had never been blistered like this before, just a bunch of raw flesh. Following the travel advice given to me to never get on a bus in Rome because the routes are so crazy you might get dropped off and never find your way back, I walked with my luggage on my back to the Gesu, walked that mile past the monumental achievements of the old Roman Empire, all of them now ruins. The flesh of my feet felt like it was on fire, from the crazy heat of the Roman summer and from the fire still stuck within my flesh from tens of miles walked or hiked each day in Spain. Ignatius' wounds, of course, were much more severe than mine. But I had a taste of what he knew with each step toward the Gesu.

Strangely, though, as I approached the Gesu, something in me knew it was Arrupe I needed to visit, more so than Ignatius and his early Jesuit companions' memorials in the chapel. I wondered why that was as I turned the corner onto that narrow street on which the Gesu rests. The car exhausts down this narrow street are always stifling, even more today during the morning rush hour. I wondered when I would be able to catch a fresh breath.

It was Arrupe who most recently encouraged an opening of the Spiritual Exercises for the world with the charism re-discovery inspired by Vatican II, and it was Arrupe who had inspired me and my freshmen-students in my high school teaching through his personal story and his challenging words. We had even named our "house" of three classes the Arrupe House in his honor. There was something about this whole thing that Ignatius had begun with his own writing of the Exercises and his Autobiography, the sadly truncated and edited story of his wild life with which nearly every high school freshman fell in love. Many of us kicked off our freshman religion classes with this book to inspire in these young men a vision for what is possible, even when lives do not begin so well. One could argue that it was the Exercises that inspired not only Ignatius' transformation from scoundrel-turned-saint but the gathering of men who would become the first Jesuits and the gathering of women who would help support and fund the growing religious order.

Just off the plane a couple of hours from visiting the places where Ignatius turned a corner on his own life, where Ignatius, a layman at the time, gave birth to the Spiritual Exercises that have been so helpful to so many for over five hundred years, I stood there at Arrupe's grave, just a few steps from Ignatius' grave, and had a hint of what might be possible with the Exercises. I hope what follows holds true — though in a very different way — to both Ignatius' 16th century vision and Arrupe's 20th century vision for the Exercises.

Could it be possible, I wondered as I stood there, to welcome a new setting of the Exercises that might gently, tenderly invite us into our own modern wildernesses, that might help us discover the living heart of the matter ... the fleshy, beating heart within us that is our life's true calling ... to know we are alive, right here, right now, to know the way love wells up within us for this life, for the people we have found ourselves loving, for the love we've been given and upon which we have thrived and the love from which we too often shy away? Could it be possible to welcome a setting that invites friends to come together and listen and converse and truly be companions — bread-breakers and bread-eaters (wheat, pita, challah or gluten-free) — on the journey together no matter from where we come, no matter our many spiritualities and life-paths and generations?

Could it be possible to welcome a new setting of the Exercises that is freed from the battle-imagery, of one standard/flag leading an army against another standard/flag for the purpose of domination, of winning a war, no matter the righteousness of the war? Could it be possible to leave behind a hierarchical approach where one who is well-versed in the Exercises leads a retreatant through the thirty-day silent retreat experience or the retreat-in-every-day-life experience that has become very popular these days? Could it be possible to trust that we will be led from within, by the inner teacher, the voice within us that has led us to life before and will certainly do so again . . . the inner teacher, the gentle voice, the one who calls us to love, no matter the costs. No matter the big names we all have developed for this "inner teacher," no matter the traditions involved with these big names, could we find a way to talk with one another and listen with one another? Indeed, could a diverse group of people come together around some open-ended questions and invitations and find the same peace of mind and perspective and life-within to "set the world on fire" as Ignatius invited his fellow companions to do as a result of discovering their own inner teachers and a love that is indeed possible through their first tastes of the Exercises or their many dippings into that deep, ever-changing well?

I know from my own experience that something happens when we gather around stories and questions and silences, something that needs very little real "work" if we pause and listen to all of them well. There's something about a story, isn't there, that unfurls something from within us, that helps the knots within us to find their way loose?

As I stood by Arrupe's tomb, I remembered talking with a Jesuit colleague about my experience of thirty days of non-directed silence and not-so-silent work among the monks at a monastery one summer. I had found something, something had found me . . . in the gathering and conversing with so many people about so many life experiences and texts and hikes and poetry and discussions (with Helen Prejean of all people, also on retreat) and good-old-monastic-work and the spans of silence when they descended around us and among us. And I posed the question to my Jesuit colleague fresh after my return to the monastery, "I know the Exercises are indeed special . . . but do you think that when we give ourselves time, without any direction except to see what passes before our eyes and ears and hearts, that we can be led to the same place that the Exercises lead us if we are open to it?" He thought about that a long time. And, despite the MANY retreats he had directed for so many people (he was often called in as one of "THE GUYS" for the Spiritual Exercises across the country), he had to admit that yes, we would be led. Such is the way of a mindful life, of trusting the inner teacher.

As I stood by Arrupe's tomb, I felt something opening within me, a lightness and a groundedness all at once. Arrupe is a man who knew well the trials of the world, and the sweetness of life even in the midst of terrible physical and emotional pain. Here was a man who ministered to murderers and rapists in the United States' maximum-security prisons and found them so soft and teary-eyed when they talked about their love for their own children. Here was a man who ministered in Japan, was interrogated as a spy and placed in solitary confinement, and once released would get together with his former prison-guards to play ping-pong and laugh and discover friendship. Here was a man who knew the awful effects of war firsthand in Hiroshima as the bombs of the United States, once his home, were dropped on his new hometown and spurred him into action to save lives with the medical school training that he had abandoned years before as not part of his calling to be a Jesuit missionary. Here was a man who ascended to the Superior General post of the Jesuits who was not afraid to rock the ship in so many ways with his speeches and actions, chief among them his "Men for Others" address of 1973. It is in this address that Arrupe told the wealthy alumni of Jesuit education that he and his fellow Jesuits had failed them because they had not inculcated in them a desire to serve the poorest of the poor on this earth nor a desire to change unjust structures that kept the rich on the path to becoming richer and the poor so often always poor and barely holding on for dear life. Here was a man who fell in love with the poor, no matter the leadership post he was given. Here was a man who found a way to set the world on fire with love even through his own illness, a stroke that changed everything for him.

As I stood there by Arrupe's tomb, I realized I only had a short time before I needed to make my way to the train station to meet up with Gillian Ahlgren and Art Dewey in Assisi. They are both former-and-forever teachers of mine and recently fellow collaborators in re-imagining the Exercises. And when we returned to Cincinnati, Karen Enriquez joined us as well as we each imagined new settings for the Exercises and tried them out with classes at Xavier University, in conversations, in texts. The conversations among the four of us were rich and challenging. As we hunkered down to wonder together, many new settings of the Exercises were born from our work . . . many I hope Gillian and Karen and Art will one day publish so that our world might, well, be. And many more must be written, so that we too might come to embrace the love that Arrupe knew despite the terrors and wildernesses of the world, so that we who have been scoundrels in our pasts might find our hearts again as Ignatius did in his transformation after his war-wounds and many, many restless nights trying to figure out what he really, really wanted with his life.

This new setting attempts three possibilities . . .

to invite the movements of the Spiritual Exercises in a small-group setting where companions come together at times to share stories and experiences with these Exercises, and

to invite people of all faiths and no faith, all questions and no questions to allow stories to be a gateway to an embodiment of soul,

to inspire others to engage the Exercises in very different ways for today's seekers who desire to set the world on fire with love.

In bringing forward this new setting of the Exercises, in doing our own inner work, in watching the clouds drift by, know that we have not found perfection . . . other than a glimpse, a taste, a feeling into our own authenticity, our own wholeness, even in the midst of the clouds. We are journeying, we are feasting and laughing and crying and growing and knowing a taste of it all, and for this time, we invite you to journey with us.

This new setting is dedicated to

Iñigo, the man who becomes Ignatius Loyola, S.J.

Pedro Arrupe, S.J.

companions in re-imagining the Spiritual Exercises in 2013 - 2014:
Gillian Ahlgren, Arthur Dewey, Karen Enriquez

companions in re-imagining the Spiritual Exercises in 2015 at VITALITY:

Shelia Barnes, Richard Bollman, S.J., Kristen Carpenter,
Tom Choquette, Tamilla Cordeiro, Coral Dill, Bailey Dixon,
Mary Duennes, Mike Eck, David Franke, Brian Geeding,
Amanda Hendricks, Jalisa Holifield, Laura & Natalie Kleinfelter,
Melanie Moon, Theresa Popelar, Bridget Rice, Brian Shircliff,
Latisha Sullivan, Maureen Sullivan-Mahoney,
Jean Marie Stross & Dan Price,
Elizabeth J. Winters Waite, Carol T. Yeazell

and all seekers the world over, all who have walked this earth, that we may know again and again the deeper roots of who we are.

Thanks to Julie Murray & Dan Hartnett, S.J., for their early conversations with Gillian, Art, and Brian. Inspiring!

Thanks to friends who read and commented upon portions of the manuscript: Mike Eck, Amy Fogelson, Ken Overberg, S.J., Jean Marie Stross, Carol T. Yeazell. Any errors that remain are Brian's.

Purchase of this book supports the work of VITALITY Cincinnati, which shares holistic self-care education neighborhood by neighborhood, person to person, and breath by breath through Greater Cincinnati. With an annual budget of $60,000, we are able to invite amazing things, many opportunities for embodiment, for knowing the heart of life, for letting ourselves begin to slow down and listen for that inner teacher inviting us to life and to life and to life, no matter the journey before us. We are grateful for your participation!

Might such a thing be possible through the Exercises, through a new setting of the Exercises? Let us come together, and let us see.

Some Preliminaries Which Might Be Helpful

A purpose of the Spiritual Exercises: Just as physical exercise creates a sound body receptive to wholeness and health, spiritual exercises are needed to free the spirit within us, so that we might more readily choose what best deepens our growth as human beings. And what we are discovering in 21st century America, as it has been well known in the East, sometimes we can combine these physical and spiritual practices for even more insight through an experience of embodiment, of soul. Where indeed is the veil that separates body from spirit ...? Perhaps they are different ways of reflecting on the same reality.

While it *might* be possible to move through the Exercises alone and at one's own pace, the experience can be so much richer with a group of people, friends on the journey, companions. This setting of the Exercises imagines a small group of companions at times gathered together for a common experience and for shared conversation and contemplation, and times for some solo exploration.

The heart of these Exercises is reflection on the past — our past and the pasts of others, the basement past of time — so that we might more readily choose a future that gives us joy and through that joy transform the world in our own unique way. Imagination is a key tool in the process. Many different types of reflection will be invited with this setting. Sometimes there is a temptation within us to know where it is all going, to see the end before we fully rely on the present. May we all begin to trust the inner teacher, what we come to know in the present moment!

That being said, here is a short sketch about what you can come to expect in the big picture of the four "weeks" or four "movements" as Ignatius imagined them. What we are doing is unearthing our past and the foundation we have inherited from our ancestors. Who knows what treasure we might bring forward from our collective past that could give us new perspective and new energy for the future? Who knows what will renew us? Who knows what we will find within us or the past itself that is ready to be aired out?

<u>Movement/Week 1</u>: A deep reflection on and marinating in moments of joy in my life. Then, briefly, a reflection on moments of pain and any unfinished business with which I might some day have the desire and energy to playfully work.

Movement/Week 2: An invitation to conversation with a wisdom teacher through story and parables and aphorisms in the parking lot of a local grocery store.

Movement/Week 3: An invitation to reflect on suffering and exile — personally and historically . . . conversations with the crucified ones, those beaten down by the powerful, of the deep past and the present. An invitation to enter into lament as a way through such exile and pain.

Movement/Week 4: An invitation to realize the depth of this life through imagining and remembering our birth and being mindful of what life we carry within us today, our own pregnancy, be it with child or idea or dream for life. An invitation to tender love.

And we move through this time together, both with the companions we have chosen for this reflection-experience and with all those with whom we journey through life. In his Autobiography, Ignatius called himself the pilgrim. No matter how deep our roots to home or family or country or tradition, we too might be wise to admit that we are pilgrims on the journey. We are on the road, we are moving. We might realize that the only real home we can truly call home is our own body, our container for this life. May we learn to live well with those who are before us each day of the journey.

No matter our professional roles in life, let us not be spiritual directors or therapists for one another, though we might begin to find ourselves listening deeply and being listened to deeply. Our job if any is to be a companion, a friend with whom we break bread (wheat, pita, challah, or gluten-free) and share food and stories and watch how this alone transforms us. There will be temptations to want to fix other people's problems, but that is their work, in their own time and way. There will be things our companions do or say about their lives that might offend us or fly in the face of a morality we try to practice. Trust that we probably offend them too in countless ways. Our job on this reflective journey, at least, is to love them just as they are and hope they find a way to love us as we are.

If someone were to tell us, "I've been thinking about that person I murdered when I was twenty and the difficult time I served in prison for it..." and your emotional and moral triggers are immediately engaged, we might take a deep breath, realize as Arrupe did during his time working in the maximum-security prisons in the United States, that this is a human being in front of us, and respond, "I've been thinking about my addictions and shortcomings too..." Practice such radical acceptance and watch how you are both transformed. Isn't it love like this that changes people, changes our relationships? In fact, as we probably know from our experience, not much else does change people. Have anyone's requests for you to change your behavior or perception of the world ever really changed your heart? Probably not. Has anyone's love and acceptance ever changed you? We can all only hope!

If we examine carefully the great stories of so many traditions that we have inherited, we might discover there are very few answers. Strange stories are told, parables and aphorisms are offered, and we are left wondering. Not much of any worth is tied up in pretty bows for us to accept at face value. Why would our ancient ancestors do this to us? Perhaps it is so that we, like them, can engage the voice of the one who whispers to us, the voice we might have heard once or twice or more often, the voice that calls us to life, to the profound sense of life we know is possible for us, for which we probably hunger. Call this inner voice that leads us to life's goodness whatever you wish, or by no name at all. If we took thirty days out of our lives for retreat, as Ignatius suggests, and prayed them without any prompts or direction, is it possible that we would be led? And the answer is "of course!" There is something within us that is wiser than we often like to remember or admit. In his early years after his own wounding, Ignatius went in search of many wise people to guide him through the inner tug-of-war of human life, but it was in his own working things out, his own wonderings and musings, that we have the Exercises we have today.

We will be wise to give each other some space in our storytelling. We do not all speak the same language, perhaps . . . even if we are all speaking "English". As we reflect upon and share stories from our own lives, we come in contact with the strange world within us, beneath us, the murky depths out of which we bloom and blossom. We come to know our inner world, strange and wonderful happenings and places that they are . . . and sometimes such happenings reach for words or concepts that are difficult to define. Some use the language of God, of various names for God, to give expression to their experiences; others might speak of synchronicity, the infinite, the deep well of the past, mystery, and more. We will all need to be prepared to listen carefully to one another as we tell our stories . . . and if we hear someone offer a story that offends us with its use of vocabulary giving shape to some important experience, we might do well to translate such experiences into our own vocabulary for a time until the storyteller's vocabulary no longer triggers in us boredom or anger or fear. Some day, we might be able to let go of different vocabularies — whether they offend or not — so that we might get a glimmer of the experience — something that might indeed be very similar to our own if we give ourselves permission to listen and watch and feel mindfully. Through storytelling, we might open ourselves to the sibling-hood of all humanity before us. Let us find out if this is indeed possible!

Much of what is offered for reflection in the 52 Invitations that follow is very open-ended, so that you and your companions can go where you most need to go that day. And of course there are many things you might want to bring to the group . . . poems to read, songs to sing, some gentle embodying meditative-movement, an open space of silence. This is after all your reflection-experience and your life. It goes without saying that you should feel free to change and adapt things offered here for your group.

Journaling, doodling, art or creative expression of so many varieties might be helpful through every invitation — as much as it is helpful to you to listen for those deeper desires within us to speak what it is we REALLY want in our lives, no matter how many more hours or years or decades we have left in this skin in which we inhabit for a time.

Ignatius designed the Spiritual Exercises with the first intent that they be offered to people through a long, silent retreat of about thirty days. Each day welcomed five different prayer opportunities and reflections, with the remaining parts of days for walks, times of contemplation in nature, rest, religious observances, etc. The director of the retreat — at first, Ignatius himself — was to watch and listen for and feel out the movements happening within the retreatant and suggest the next prayer opportunity needed. Some people, he felt, would benefit only from an extended experience of the first week/movement, others might complete all four weeks though maybe need an extended journey through one of the weeks until some special inner-treasure might became apparent. The key thing we might read here from Ignatius' own annotations about the Exercises is that they are malleable, offered as a way to invite the retreatant to even more life, a deeper and more profound awareness of life.

Eventually, Ignatius came to realize that even people who were not able to put their lives to a thirty-day halt could benefit from the Exercises, so he began adapting them for people who might have, say, an hour a day to reflect and grow through the inner-terrain in which the Exercises begin to offer a map. And these invitations that follow might be beneficial to someone who might only have an hour a day — if even that — or for someone who has all the time in the world for reflection, even thirty solid days. Maybe before you move from invitation to invitation, ask yourself if you're ready to move on. Sit with that question. Rest here awhile, a few moments, with that question. After all, what is the rush? Trust whatever your deepest guts tell you ... to stay here with one of the invitations for a day or a few days or perhaps even not at all. After all, that is the invitation of the Spiritual Exercises ... to begin to listen for Wisdom within us, often a quieter voice than all the others that blare their way through our everyday lives.

We have left much space on these pages open, blank, for your notes, ideas, suggestions, prompts. We have resisted the custom to italicize "Spiritual Exercises" (and for that matter, Ignatius' Autobiography which was spoken to one of his companions and only later recorded as the "book" we have inherited) because it was perhaps Ignatius' own desire that they not be books but an ongoing, building, growing collection of ideas, suggestions for reflection and for opening up our lives. May you please be so bold as to improve this "text" with your own movements of soul and then share them with the world!

With the italicized portions of the text that follow, it might be helpful to have companions take turns with each invitation to read aloud the meditations and stories offered there. Again, do whatever is helpful.

In any case, get a move on, as many wisdom teachers remind us ... but go slowly and mindfully too. It's the only way to smell the sweetness of the flowers and know why bees spend their days in search of them.

Preliminary Meeting Before Setting Out Together with These Invitations

If you do indeed move through these invitations together, it seems wise before we begin to gather together and offer to one another the opportunity of our friendship and companionship through these invitations and our hopes and dreams for what these invitations might awaken in us. Maybe ask too, of one another, anything that you feel might be needed during your time together . . . "would you listen to me and see if you notice what it seems like I am really passionate about when I tell my stories?" or "if my tears find me again about my recent loss, would you please remind me to . . ." or whatever it is that we know we might need before we walk these invitations together.

It would be nice for the gathering to be in person, though maybe if you're using some upcoming vacation time to actually live together for these first few invitations and now you live far apart, perhaps a conference/on-line call together might be a possibility, one to two weeks before you begin together this opportunity, the first invitation . . . maybe over dinner at someone's house, some place and time that you can linger together, take some time to get to know one another and one another's hopes and anticipations about the retreat by answering these questions with one another and any others you feel important:

What is leading you right now to pursue these invitations at this point in your life?

Please tell one story from your life where you really experienced the goodness of life.

Can we find a way to listen to and for one another that might even help us get to know our own deeper longings for life? Can our own telling of stories and listening to others' stories help us to begin to know a love of life that we might have only glimpsed in all our years?

As we enjoy and practice storytelling with one another, can we give ourselves permission to begin to appreciate the texture and terrain and sound and feeling within stories? Can we begin to know this world, this special world that lingers both above and beneath the surface of a well-told story?

It seems important to have this conversation with our companions many days before we "officially" begin . . . to let some time move under our feet and some dreams to churn up the rich soil within us in the days leading up to the beginning with Invitation 1.

In moving through these invitations, though, the most important thing to do, of course, is to listen in on the rich life within us, within our own self and within our companions. Let the inner teacher lead you to where your deepest longing is calling you to be, and if these invitations that follow are helpful in that listening . . . well, great. And if not . . . know we walk with you as you set out to compose your own!

Invitation 1: Arriving

If you are beginning these invitations at home or at a retreat-center or on a vacation, let's give ourselves permission to arrive in every way. Physically, Emotionally, Spiritually, Wholly.

Check-in/get unpacked, take a walk, explore the surroundings with new eyes and ears and skin. Even if you've lived here your whole life, take a nap, begin to slow down, to rest, to arrive. If the weather or anything else prevents such exploration, perhaps sit by a window and slow down awhile to the life you see out there or even close your eyes and imagine your surroundings, even if you are here for the first time.

Maybe find a space in your room that will begin to be helpful for you to wait quietly and listen during these invitations . . . maybe a desk or a chair or a special blanket or pillow or meditation cushion.

Maybe you'd like the space to be nice but relatively empty . . . or maybe you'd like some special things there that are important to you . . . artwork, symbols, photographs of loved ones, paints and journal and things that help with your creative expression. Maybe just a simple notebook and pen are all you feel you need.

Do what feels right in creating your space — and of course, give yourself permission to change it up at any time as it is helpful for you.

Maybe sit here for a few minutes, journal about those hopes and dreams you have for this retreat-experience, these invitations. You had the opportunity to voice them with your companions — at least with yourself — a few days ago. As you sit here now, what comes to mind? What bubbles up from within you that might seem important now?

Take some time now, and even if nothing comes immediately or at all, let that be alright for now.

Invitation 2: New Rhythm

With each of these invitations, maybe you would benefit most by reading them slowly to yourself before going out and experiencing them, or maybe if your companions have gathered together, you would benefit from someone from the group reading the italicized portions of the invitation below slowly and simply; anyone not reading might want to close their eyes or meditate . . . perhaps even let these invitations be a guided meditation of sorts . . . again, whatever is most helpful.

Take some time to walk slowly this morning. Make your way to a park or some natural area, whether you find yourself in the country or the city or some in between spot. Even a nice patch of grass or a tree or two can do. Find a nice spot on which to sit, to rest. If it's not possible to sit outside — maybe it's terribly cold or you are not feeling well or whatever prevents you — you might consider sitting by a large window, maybe hold a cup of tea and just observe from there. Or even find an indoor plant, water it, and listen to the water soaking into the soil, into the roots, linger, wait here mindfully, take it all in.

Wherever you are, take some time to observe the natural world around you . . . notice the non-linear lines of nature, of trees and grass and plants and flowers . . . all of them perfect in their own way yet non-conforming to any immediately noticeable pattern. Take in the beauty of it all. Close your eyes for some time. Listen for all the sounds surrounding you. Listen for sounds in the far distance, maybe even of cars whizzing by, of children playing, of conversations. Let every sound relax you even more.

Listen for sounds a little closer to you, sounds maybe of birds or insects playing and moving, maybe of the breeze running through the trees or the grass, the sounds of water. Listen deeply and drink it all in.

Listen then for sounds within your own body, of a meal being digested, of air moving through your mouth or nostrils, maybe you can even hear or feel your own heart beating within your chest or another part of your body. Take in every sound just as it is . . . let every sound relax you even more with little need to identify any of them or judge them. Allow yourself, give yourself permission to take in this symphony of sound.

After some time, let every sense pull you into your experience of this moment. Smell, touch, taste the air, let your eyes and ears find joy in what happens here.

Let your eyes be dazzled by all the colors and different shades of colors that surround you. Watch how they change in the light and the shade.

Maybe you can even imagine what is going on in that tremendous world below the surface of the grass or ground on which you rest . . . the earthworms and nematodes moving deeply through the soil and regenerating the earth. How large this tract of grass or ground — an entire world or continent for an ant!

Take time to notice how every one of these creatures and grasses and wind and sun all move in their own way, how nature has its own rhythms, its own way of proceeding through life, through time. What can you take in of the beauty of this rhythm?

As you do all of this, you might begin to notice memories, dreams, moments of your life bubbling up from the surface of your within. Whatever they are, let them be for awhile, no need to sort them or judge them.

Rest here awhile . . . .

When it's time to return back to the place where you are staying, walk slowly, mindfully, notice gently your steps, where you can feel the weight shift in your feet, in your body, in your arms as they swing with each step in their own natural way.

What has happened for you here? Perhaps journal about it, and later find some time to share your story with someone and maybe your companions on this journey will have a story too to offer you.

Invitation 3: Mandala Exercise

Draw or trace or even free-hand a fairly large circle in the center of a large piece of paper. Have plenty of pastels or colored pencils or crayons available, enough so that everyone can take a large handful to be used personally in the activity.

With all of the colors randomly spilled out, reach into the pile and grab a generous handful without any forethought.

Find some space for yourself within the room and rest here awhile with the empty page. Maybe simply look at the circle or meditate or move as you feel called to gently move. And then with colors in hand, simply react to the page. Mindlessly, reach into your small pile and take one color and scribble, make some design . . . do all of this by reacting. This is an exercise where you let your guts rule and let your mind quiet as much as possible. Have no preferences on which color you pick up next, no preferences on what it does on the paper. Stay in the lines or move outside the lines of the circle. Just let yourself react, and continue to react until you feel like you are finished.

If you finish before others, just take some time to look at your mandala, your design. Turn the paper this way and that, just noticing. We'll work with these designs in some invitations to come. No need to judge any of it, just let it be. Maybe take some joy in the fact that you gave yourself some time to create something — however creative you feel you are.

Invitation 4: Joy

A meditation . . .

Today, take some time for a slow walk, or if that is not comfortable, sit again by a window and slow down for awhile. Bring along a journal or at least a piece of paper on which to write. Maybe find a spot like the other day where you can sit down and rest for some time. Today, we are invited to remember moments of joy in life, moments when we were having so much fun we could barely stand it, moments when we felt so, so, alive! These could be big moments like weddings or births of children or graduations. They could be simple moments of everyday life that catch us almost unexpectedly and upon which we depend . . . like watching the flowers or the grass in the wind the other day, or sloppy wet kisses from children in our lives, that first taste of ice cream on a hot summer day, the feeling of a lover close to us while we sleep, the feeling of watching the moon and stars in the night sky. Please create a list of all of these experiences, all of these moments of joy from your own life. The list can be as long as you like it to be — maybe at least ten things would be helpful for later invitations.

As you create your handwritten list or collage of memories, become aware of any feelings from these memories.

Know too that sometimes when we remember moments of joy in our lives, moments of pain or moments that feel undone or incomplete might bubble up from within too. No worries about these now. Just let them be. We'll get a chance to work with those another day. For today, let joy rule, and when something not so joyful comes up, take a few deep breaths to acknowledge these memories and maybe even a tinge of the feeling that is attached to them, and then let the memory and the feeling pass. If this is difficult, come back to the present, notice yourself here in nature, alive in this larger world, feel yourself breathing here, sitting here. Take in the joys of nature that you experienced yesterday and let those feelings of life's goodness springboard you back into other memories of joy and happiness.

Have you ever seen small children — four, five, six years old — when someone tells them, "We're going to go get ice cream!"? Assuming these children like ice cream, what do the children do? Notice how the joy within each child cannot be contained. The child's little body begins to shake with excitement, and each child begins running around the room with the others — long before the ice cream is even tasted. Such is joy. It spills over, it spills out of us, and is even contagious as everyone else in the room becomes excited too.

So let your list begin, and let yourself stew in this goodness. Even if some of the memories on your list might have been forbidden at the time or are taboo to some, let them be. It is your list, your life, your experience! Remember . . . feel this joy in your body, in your memory, even if we have to wait all day and night for it to make itself known.

Later on, with your companions, or anyone you might encounter today, choose one of these moments from life and tell the story. Notice what happens within you as you tell it, and notice what happens for the person receiving your story. Sometimes watching the eyes of the storyteller can help to draw you in even more to the scene of the story.

What is it that we know about joy?

Invitation 5: Traipsing Over the Mandala's Terrain

Place the mandala that you created in Invitation 3 in your hand. Absorb the colors, the strange shapes, the texture of the pastels/paints, the lines inside the circle and any outside the circle. There will always be temptations to judge our work, but this is not an exercise that involves any judgment. Simply be present to the colors and designs on the page. Turn your mandala every different direction. What do you see? What do you experience?

After maybe 3 - 4 minutes of sitting in silence just looking at your own mandala, read to yourself or have someone read this invitation to you . . .

Take a moment to place your mandala nearby you, and if it feels good for you, close or at least soften your eyes. Feel your body in the chair or on the ground, whatever feels right for you. With each exhale, see if you can feel your body relaxing . . . maybe in your shoulders or neck, maybe you can feel your hips letting go, maybe even your feet feel both lighter and heavier on the floor. Take some time to enjoy this. (pause)

Imagine the mandala you have created is an enormous field . . . maybe as large as one or two soccer/football fields in size. As you look down underneath and around your feet on this mandala, you see the colors and shapes and textures and lines of your mandala. They of course are larger now.

Take some time on your own to begin wandering along this field, along this mandala. Notice any feelings you might experience as you walk along.

Are there any places on this massive mandala where you feel so free that you want to run or jump or play? (long pause)

Are there any places on this mandala where you feel so comfortable that you could sit down and rest, maybe even take a nap? (long pause)

Are there any places on this mandala where you feel not so free — maybe you feel confused or lost or unsure? (long pause)

Maybe there are even some places on the mandala where you feel anxious or angry or afraid?

Take some time to wander around your mandala, and notice any feelings that arise. You are safe here, this is your experience, your opportunity to explore — so any feelings that come up, you know that you have the support of the group both to enjoy them and to feel them as they are. Take some time for yourself right now just to be here on your mandala.

(after maybe another 3-4 minutes) After taking some time to explore your mandala, I invite you to slowly begin making your way back to the place from which you began on your mandala. Once you have arrived at that beginning spot, turn and look over the whole terrain, the whole circle. Take all the time you need in the next minute or so to do that.

(after about a minute) And once you have arrived back to that spot and taken that last full look, I invite you to take a few cleansing breaths, if that feels good for you, and then begin opening your eyes and silently come back to the group.

Place your mandala in your hands again and take another look, turn it this way and that, continuing to explore . . . and then, if it feels right, turn your attention to your journal to answer three questions:

1. Pick one or two places on your mandala where you felt incredible joy or happiness or felt so comfortable you could take a nap there. In a short paragraph, describe the color or the design and briefly write about why you felt so comfortable there.

2. Pick one or two places on your mandala where you might have felt confused or anxious or maybe even angry or fearful or sad. Again, describe the color or the design and briefly write a short paragraph or two about why you might have felt that way there.

3. In a single sentence, write about what you learned about yourself from this mandala exercise.

Consider keeping this mandala in your reflection/meditation area or near your bed to continue to explore what it might offer you in these next days.

Invitation 6: Knowing Deeply These Moments of Joy

With your list or collage of joy-moments you made with Invitation 4, take some time to be with joy . . .

Let's take a moment or two to choose one of those moments, perhaps the moment that brings you the most joy in remembering. As you relax here, let that moment play out in your imagination.

(move slowly through all of these . . .)

Notice the people, the things that you see there in that moment.

Notice the expressions on people's faces, the ways they carry themselves and respond to one another.

Notice the sounds, the voices that you hear.

Perhaps there is a particular smell or taste associated with this moment.

What does the air feel like on your skin?

Maybe you can even remember the feeling in your guts from this moment. Take some time to let it all come to you as you remember.

After taking some time with one of these moments of joy, perhaps turn your attention to your journal and write anything else that comes to you about that moment. Mine the gold that is there. What is there for you to discover here?

If it feels right for you, consider . . .

writing a poem or a short play/screenplay that might help describe this feeling of joy;

drawing or painting — maybe a picture of the event or a symbol about joy;

composing a song or a dance.

Do anything that helps you to know so well this feeling of joy ... a foundation of these Spiritual Exercises .... Maybe even something from the mandala exercise in the previous invitation will help you know something, remember something.

Whatever you do, stay with this feeling for awhile. **This is so important that if you are not able for whatever reason to remember or feel this joy, it would be best not to move on to the next invitations. Let knowing such joy as this be a tap-root for all of the invitations to come.**

Even if we don't think of ourselves as creative people ("I'm not an artist!"), sometimes by engaging our reflections creatively and imaginatively — even journaling in different colors — unfurls tremendous power and insight in us.

Invitation 7: When Joy, Life Has Been Interrupted . . .

Consider resting in the quiet for some time, simply being mindful of your body . . . feel your breath coming into your body, that slight pause between inhale and exhale, and then the breath leaving your body . . . see if you can tune into this rhythm the body has, much like the ocean's waves.

Sometimes our bodies have a way of telling us what we need to know, especially regarding those moments in life where we have been interrupted, disrupted, moments when life has been overwhelming, difficult, painful, torn, whatever.

Consider placing your hands on or near your knees, feeling your feet well-supported on the ground as you rest in a chair or on the ground itself. As your hands rest on or near your knees here for awhile, whatever is most comfortable for you, perhaps you can feel your heart beating so far away here on your knees . . .

As we are invited to move through our body, to hold each part of our body, maybe it would be helpful to ask, "What do I need to know here? What do I need to know about my life through this part of my body?" Maybe whatever bubbles up from the surface of within might be helpful as we contemplate these moments that may have interrupted joy in our lives. Take some time with this exercise. Let it unfold.

So, from our knees, let our hands move to our hips for awhile . . .

then onto our guts/navel . . . (pause)

then onto our heart/rib-basket . . . (pause)

then onto our shoulders/neck . . . if it's not comfortable to have your hands there, maybe simply imagine your hands resting there . . . (pause)

same with your head . . . (pause)

anywhere else on your own body you'd like to explore . . . (what might your body have to say here, and here, and here?) . . .

After you've had some time with this, consider journaling anything from this exercise that might be helpful for you, before we turn our attention to this meditation:

Today, we are invited to create a list of these moments of interruption. They could be moments of personal challenge, moments of pain or loss, moments of trauma for yourself or someone you love or even the discovery that someone's life in the world has been made very difficult by some catastrophe or person or agenda. Or moments of anger or fear or anxiety, moments when we might have caused someone pain or thrown a wrench into someone's dreams, even moments with which you still don't know what to do. Let them all come, let them all be listed here today, either by word or symbol or drawing. There might be some unfinished business with these moments, some grief that wants to be expressed through tears or journaling. That's all good. Let those feelings be. Sometimes in giving ourselves permission to feel them, their attachment to our lives changes, and they no longer have quite the hold on our lives that they sometimes do.

As much as our journal might be an aid for us, it might be even more helpful to have a friend who can sit by us, someone with whom to be with one another in these moments. Or even someone you know you can call, someone you know who will offer her/his ear anytime.

As we remember these moments of disruption and pain, especially if we feel overwhelmed or burdened by them, it could be helpful to seek some professional help, a trained counselor who might help us untangle the yarn of life. Perhaps we know someone who is a trained and trusted ear, and if not, there are so many resources available to us, even special groups devoted to listening to and seeing one another through the tough times. There's even

1 (800) 273-8255
National Suicide Prevention Lifeline
Hours: 24 hours, 7 days a week
Languages: English, Spanish
Website: www.suicidepreventionlifeline.org

or many other local or online resources who might be helpful.

Know that there is someone who wants to lend you support if you reach out.

If there is someone with whom we are moving through these invitations, a companion or conversation-partner of sorts, it can be helpful to simply let each other know where you will be for one another if you need someone to be close by . . . sometimes even knowing there is someone who is also doing this inner work or being mindful of us makes all the difference.

As painful as some of these moments might be, Ignatius reminds us that there is some gift in all of these moments, even the ones we certainly wouldn't want to experience again. Every moment of our lives has helped us to arrive right where we are here and now, on this retreat, in these moments of reflection. And what a good place to be here. Every moment has helped us to grow to be the good people we are now. That alone might be the gift.

We might want to journal about these moments, or simply create a list that we can look back to throughout these exercises. Do whatever feels right for you. Know that in the next invitation, we will explore Ignatius' life, one of many tragic interruptions throughout his life, even at a young age.

Invitation 8: Ignatius' story . . . of interruption

If you've never read Ignatius Loyola's Autobiography, we all highly recommend it. In it, Ignatus calls himself "the pilgrim" . . . almost as if he knew just how much his journey would be tied up with our own in some way. Even five hundred years later. Like some kind of archetype of a seeker, perhaps.

I had the opportunity to read and discuss this autobiography yearly for fifteen years with high school freshmen . . . with three classes a year, that was forty-five times. And I was always amazed that his story could touch these young, wise souls so much. Perhaps we all know something of the trauma and the growth that Ignatius experienced. Life is not always easy.

The one we know as Ignatius was earlier known as Iñigo, his childhood name. And perhaps it's wise to let us know this man through that name, Iñigo, a name he answered to long before his fame as framer of Exercises and Founder/Superior General of the Society.

Sadly, much of the Autobiography about his years as Iñigo was probably edited out, especially his early years, his days as a ruffian and wild boy. But many biographies about him provide ample evidence of his ways before being wounded in battle and his whole vision of his life being called into question. Ronald Modras' *Ignatian Humanism* (2004) has a wonderfully honest portrait of this troubled soul.

Iñigo's is a story of a life. There will, I'm sure, be moments that make you squirm, that contradict what you expect out of a "saint," out of anybody. See if you can reserve judgment until the end or even not at all. It is out of this life that Ignatius, Iñigo, crafts the Spiritual Exercises that have helped so many, that have inspired this journey that we have undertaken together, dear companion. See if you can be at peace with what has happened for him.

Our own journey is incomplete as well . . . just waiting for us to make the next simple or bold move.

As you read the very abbreviated story below, perhaps see if you can pause and feel each moment . . .

Iñigo was born into a very large family, the eleventh child of his mother . . . "of his mother" because his father had children with other women as well, apparently a bit of a tradition in this wealthy family. Their home was a castle, their family respected even by the Spanish royalty of the day through their loyal service in war and in peace. A few of Iñigo's older brothers died in battle.

His family was Basque, from a region of modern-day Spain where warriors from long ago made it very difficult for the Romans to come in and do as they pleased. Indeed, there is a reason that this part of Spain still retained its own language — Rome was not quite as successful here as elsewhere in subjugating these Basques as they were just about everywhere else. Imagine the pride that must have coursed through their veins, these Basques. Perhaps even a machismo that demanded a response of its men, to continue to defend their honor as their ancestors had done against emboldened attacks and attempts to alter their culture, to put them down.

Iñigo's mother died when he was young, shortly after he was born. Imagine what her life was like, especially knowing that her husband was sleeping around. Imagine what it would have been like to raise eleven children, and to have to bury a few of them who had died in battle. Imagine her terrible grief . . . about many things.

Imagine what it would have been like for Iñigo to grow up in such a household, both before and after his mother's death . . . what it would have been like to have been raised by older sisters.

Imagine the stories that were important to him and to all boys of his family's stature, the knightly romances that were told and read and lived out . . . tales of knights who fought for honor, who defended the royal family from whom everyone (supposedly) received financial benefits and diplomatic protection, who (supposedly) protected the weak from the forces of nature that could cripple . . . armies, bandits, monsters and more. Like any good nobleman who fought in the royal army, Iñigo's brothers would have taught young Iñigo how to fight with the weapons that every male of stature carried . . . sword, dagger, knives, maybe more.

As he matured into adolescence, Iñigo became known for his bravery in his hometown, and perhaps for his pranks. Following in the footsteps of his father, Iñigo was well-known among the young ladies, and they were probably greatly attracted to him. As he reflects in the Autobiography, he was known for his looks, was meticulous about his long hair and even his nails. Imagine what people must have said about him, what they whispered as he walked their streets. "There he goes. Did you hear what he did this time?"... some little story of a prank he pulled or some foolishly daring adventure he and his buddies went after ... probably all to woo the young women of their young lives.

In today's terms, perhaps we could imagine him to be the guy on the team who always brags after the game about all he did. "Did you see me? Did you see how sweet I was? Yeah, you threw me the ball, but did you see how I dove for it and caught it and got up and ran it forty yards for the touchdown? That's how good I am. Yeah, you're involved and all — but, let's be honest, nothing happens without me. I mean, could anyone even touch me?" And always said just loud enough for a young lady to overhear and admire him, and if he was fortunate enough, to want him enough that he might lure her into his web.

Iñigo mentions that he had great feelings for a certain unnamed lady, perhaps someone of a rank above him. Maybe even the young princess that he might have spied as his family and the other nobility were called forward at the royal court for the annual appearance, assemblies to remember the hierarchy and patriarchy, the systems to which they had all pledged their lives. What crazy possibilities might have entered young Iñigo's mind as he plotted just how he might catch the attention of this certain young lady. But until then, he, uh, practiced with the young ladies of the town.

Those in his family raising him decide to ship him off to the local duke so that young Iñigo may find his way in the world — and maybe to settle him down a little too. As the youngest in the family, he had no claim on the inheritance, no claim on the wealth of castle Loyola. So, in the service of the duke, he was trained as an emissary, a diplomat. But he was called into battle too.

Imagine what might have run through his mind during his daydreams, his night-dreams. "Just what can I do to make her fall in love with me ...?"

And when even a diplomat like Iñigo was called into battle against the French, when they all were holed up in Pamplona with many of his countrymen and many, many, many more Frenchmen crossing over the hillside, all for the annual border-skirmish battle where the French apparently meant business this year, Iñigo's twenty-sixth year of life ... imagine the voices of the Pamplona towns-folk. "Please, please surrender, all of you, that we all might live! Yes, yes, you warriors might be jailed, but His Majesty will bail you out and we will keep our homes. Please, please surrender!" they probably begged. And how all of the officers must have sympathized, how they agreed at first to a surrender as they imagined the possible casualties of being so terribly outnumbered.

And how Iñigo must have seized the moment . . . how he saw this as his moment to secure forever the good graces of the crown, especially that certain young lady that had been the focus of his daydreams. "If I can get these men to fight with me, and we win just like our ancestors did against the armies of Rome, the greatest empire of the day, and I am presented not only to the local duke but to the whole royal court as the one who inspired these cowards to fight, well, this . . ."

Imagine the speech he must have offered, the home-grown hero speech we all know from movies of our time, a speech that rouses within the nationalistic fervor that can get anyone to fight for honor, for truth, for country and one another. And fight they did, valiantly, though only for a short time . . . until a French cannonball blasted Iñigo's leg and then bounced off the other one.

Imagine him there on the ground in the most horrible pain he had ever known, his one leg in shards there before him, the possibility of bleeding-out more real with every moment. His fellow warriors all surrendered when they saw their inspiration down for the count. In marched the French, and in times of honor like these, you can imagine the conversation . . . "Why did you even try to fight us — you were so vastly outnumbered!"

"Well, it was this man right here, Iñigo, he so inspired us."

"We will make sure one as brave as this is cared for." And the French made sure that Iñigo was shipped home, a procession of honor whereby he might eventually be home to die in peace if he was lucky, or live as a crippled war veteran with all the glamour and riches and pain and discomfort that accompanies such a life at that time.

Imagine what went through his mind on those bumpy roads toward his home, what pain he endured as the shattered bones of his leg were jolted with every bump. Surely roads of this period weren't flat like ours today, were they? Imagine what his family must have experienced when they first saw him so close to death — another one about to succumb to death just like their older brothers, his older son.

Maybe try to get only a glimpse of the pain Iñigo must have experienced as the doctors of his day opened the wounded mess of his leg and tried to reassemble it to heal, and their discovery that a few of the bones would need to be whacked and re-broken because they had begun to heal on his journey home — and not in any way that would let him walk again. And all of this without any pain killers, without any anesthesia. And the story he tells of never crying out once during the surgeries or after them ... what was he thinking? Why did he hold back that cry? One more stroke of bravado? machismo?

Imagine the terrible days and nights as Iñigo fought off infection after infection, doctor after doctor proclaiming he was lucky to have lived this long with such a wound. And then just when the haze of sickness had left him and he was well enough to converse, one of the first things he asks is for that unsightly bump on his leg to be sawed off. While the ladies might swoon over my hero-status as a war veteran, imagine him surmising, they would surely react to seeing or having to touch that awful bump on my leg where the set-bones had healed a bit awry.

Imagine the doctors' faces when they say to him, "You think you have known pain thus far?! Sawing off the bump will be far worse than anything you have already experienced." But in his vanity, Iñigo demanded it. And so they did what he asked, without a single cry from him as they ground down that bony outgrowth without a cry or a protest of any sort. He just clenched his fists and took it.

And then after all of this madness, wonder what he began thinking about, what kinds of things flitted through his brain without any effort. Was he sad about his wounding? Did he experience grief for what he thought his life would be? Did he even know what he really wanted — in his twenty-six years?

Recovery took a long time. A long, long time. Imagine him having fantasies about that certain lady, about what their lives together might be like, about all the ways he was attracted to her. Imagine the excitement coursing through him.

But even those fantasies were not enough to stave off his boredom. These were not days of push-button entertainment . . . no cable-television or on-demand movies, no recorded music, no computer-generated games, barely a culture of books. Probably tired of the people who had become his post-war conversation companions —family, friends, neighbors as he recovered at home — Iñigo asked for some of those knightly romances that had been his favorites as a kid. Maybe there would be a line or a gesture I could glean, imagine him saying, that would help me find favor with that certain lady if I have the chance. Imagine his excitement, to know that he had had a taste of such adventure in battle, as bitter as his current lot was. He would have tales to tell her, to tell everyone.

But there were no books like these in the house. Only two books about the lives of the saints and the life of Jesus.

Imagine the eye-roll when these were brought to him. He was raised to be religious — nearly everyone of Spain was — but what good would that do him when he's immobilized in his bed day after long day, all in an attempt to regain his health, his life? Besides, what kind of adventure is there in pious, religious life?

But in his boredom, he began reading those books. Surely he had heard these stories before — maybe now with a certain openness that before his battle-adventures was not quite possible. He read of Francis of Assisi, like Iñigo from a wealthy family, like him drawn into war, like him teetering on the edge of death as a result of war and rotting in the enemy's underground jail cell for months. And when he had regained some semblance of health, Francis would wander down in the valley, his sanctum outside the protecting walls of the city. To be outside the city walls during this era, any era, carried great risk. You never know whom you might encounter. And one day, Francis met a beggar, a leper. He had seen lepers before, of course, and ran from them like any decent human being would do. But now something in him paused, looked the young very sick man in the eyes, considered him for the first time. Francis knew something of pain, of trauma, of life-destroying illness. And something in him wanted to touch this broken young man, this leper, no matter the costs.

It wasn't long after this that Francis decided he could not live like his wealth-growing family did, his father the luxury cloth merchant of the town who owned some of that land outside the city gates where Francis met the leper. When he protests to his father that he wants no part of the family wealth and no part of the family business, that what he really wants is to live down there with the beggars and the lepers and the supposed low-life outside the walls of the city, Francis' father locks him in a cage of sorts in the family home until his cries so upset his mother that she lets him out. And what does Francis do but bee-line it to his father, make his protest by the bishop's chair for all to see, and take off all that was his father's. Francis removes his clothes, renounces his claim to the inheritance, and walks naked out of the city to gather with others who wanted no part in the economic structure that was growing every day in Italy ... lepers, rejects, prostitutes (to whom he might have once paid a visit), etc. And Francis finds joy here, in the so-called dangerous life outside the walls with these so-called dangerous people in whom he discovers love for the first time.

Imagine Iñigo reading Francis' story. Iñigo knew too something of that kind of bravery, that kind of courage when everyone is watching, his own amazing speech to sway everyone to fight. Pshaw — if Francis can get his name in the book for something like this, well then I can too, we might imagine Iñigo saying to himself. And all of these other people — these so-called saints — I can do better than them when it comes to adventure!

And just as he begins making plans in his mind for this adventure and that, all of these attempts he will want to make when he is fully recovered, all to get his own name in the book with the likes of Francis and all the greats, imagine how Iñigo's mind turns back to the lady, to the castle that he and she will one day inhabit with their many children, the tremendous happiness that will be his, theirs.

And so the tug began . . . every day, every hour. One hour he desires the life of adventure like Francis found outside the walls, another hour dreaming of the lady and their life together in the castle.

Days upon days upon days of this, of noticing these feelings he wrestles within himself. What do I want? What do I want? What do I really want?

And eventually, as he gained again the ability to walk through the halls of his family-castle, he had to admit that he did not really know. How his eyes must have gazed at and craved the countryside, the fresh air outside the walls of his own family, his own boyhood home. Maybe once I get out of here for awhile, he must have thought, I can finally put the matter to rest and figure out what I really want.

When he is well enough, he tells his brother that he must go on a journey — um, to see the duke. His brother agrees that this is wise, that war-ravaged Iñigo can go claim the no-small reward for being a war-veteran in the service of the duke. But something about Iñigo is different, and his brother knows it, begs him not to throw his life away as Iñigo hobbles around the castle and his brother chases him with argument after argument. What is it that his brother must have known about his little brother? What was it he had witnessed changing so much to worry that he would throw it all away so quickly?

But Iñigo knows he must go — and not just to see the duke. He must figure it out one way or another. A long walk will do. A pilgrimage to Spain's most famous site for pilgrims — no small journey from his Loyola castle.

After visiting the duke and receiving a substantial payment, Iñigo asks for a statue to be erected in honor of another Lady, the Virgin Mary. And then he makes the long journey from Loyola, across northern Spain's mountainous roads to the Serrated Mountain — Montserrat — where another statue of the Lady is well known and visited, the Black Madonna with child. What is rather strange though is that Iñigo takes with him his armor from battle, his sword. And like any good knight before battle, Iñigo stands at attention all night before that Lady, only in the morning slipping out before anyone might make a big deal about it, his sword and armor left behind at the Lady's feet.

What stirred in him to so symbolically leave behind the symbols of his old life?

He makes his way down the mountain to the next town, Manresa. He thinks it a nice enough place to spend a long weekend, just enough time he thinks to figure out what to do next.

But he stayed there much longer than a weekend — almost a year, in fact, as he tried to make sense of what he really wanted, what he desired most in his life. How his past must have sickened him, his life of wealth and ease as the youngest son of a rich family, of all the childish pranks he had pulled, of the women he had used for his own pleasure, of the posturing he had perfected to gain the favor of person after person after person, all to get what he really wanted, the hand of the lady of his dreams, their new castle, their children, their life of honor and ease and . . . whatever.

He has a hard time at Manresa as he reflects on what is happening within him, as he travels the inner-world of what he assumes to be the damned, the inner-world of all the disruptions he had experienced, the early death of his mother, the wild life of his childhood in a house without a real parent, the crazy party-life of him and his friends, all the terrible things he had done to get his way . . . to get whatever he wanted to eat or drink or do or have sex with, his time serving the duke in a number of roles to attempt to carve out a life, his terrible wounding that changed it all.

He seeks out so many people with whom to converse, so many people whom he hopes will tell him like it is spiritually, people who will help him navigate this horror of his inner life of traumatic memories, of desires that contradict and make no sense . . . of life with the lady and the castle (a desire he claims lacks the luster it once had), of life living in a cave and meditating and praying (as he was that year in Manresa), of maybe even death by suicide if this craziness in his head did not soon sort itself out.

But we know it did sort itself out. And we know from his Autobiography that he did indeed seek out so many people with whom to get the answers . . . only to discover that the answers were within. And he befriended woman after woman after woman, Isabel Roser among them, and none of them for sexual relationship and domination as he once had, but now one of friendship. Many years after these hard days of inner-work, Iñigo with his new gang who gathered around him just as they gathered around Francis for a new way, founded a house for former prostitutes who were trying to find their feet on a new path.

And he finds that he can sleep anywhere now, under a bridge, in a cave, in a field. The world is his home.

And the boy who once probably was well-versed in making others cry now cries at the drop of a hat . . . when he is meditating/praying, when life wells up within him at the utter beauty of it all, when he finds himself — gulp — grateful for the cannonball.

What had gotten into Iñigo?

That in his woundings, his interruptions, our woundings and interruptions . . . is such love as this possible . . . ?

Invitation 9: Sitting with Ignatius

Iñigo's life was one of disruption, of interruption. Perhaps it would be helpful to spend some time with his story in silence, maybe with your journal.

As you reflect on Ignatius' moments of interruption and your own moments, what do you discover about them?

Have any of them been caused by choices you made?

Have any of them been caused by the choices of others?

Have any of them been brought about by some natural disaster?

Have any of them been the work of larger forces that might be difficult to pinpoint . . . forces of the economy, a corporate structure, dynamics of power or politic that are difficult to understand?

Journal about anything that comes to you about these moments of interruption. What is there to learn here about ourselves, about how human beings and life can sometimes be?

Invitation 10: Sitting with Ourselves

Today, consider sitting in the quiet for awhile. Come back to your breath, enjoying the sound of the breath coming into your body and the breath rolling out of your body. Come back to something as simple as these sensations that awaken in us when we mindfully breathe through this body we have been given . . . maybe even allow ourselves to be breathed.

If it feels right for you, place a hand on your heart. Feel the amazing beating of your own heart. Its rhythm cannot be copied by anyone or anything, its own unique patterning, music.

And if it feels right, keep one hand here on your heart and another hand (physically or imaginatively) on your belly, on your guts. Scientists tell us today that there as many or even more neurons here in the guts as there are in your brain. Amazing. And yet maybe we know this from our own experience, our trusting of gut-reactions, intuition, inner knowledge, much like the ancestors did before us.

What might your heart have to say to your guts today?

What might your guts have to say to your heart?

Maybe as we sit here awhile, consider the many desires you have . . . desires as simple as what tastes good to you to eat or drink, desires for all kinds of things . . . relationships, experiences, affection, freedom from something, new horizons, and on and on and on.

Feel no rush to try to figure out things over a long-weekend like Iñigo hoped he could at Manresa. Let's simply see if we can just let them be for a time as we sit here. Maybe even journal about them for awhile, maybe even consider how each particular desire makes you feel as you consider it. Know that there are no bounds to what we desire. See if you can leave behind for a time what might seem like categories like "appropriate desire" and whatever we or someone else might deem inappropriate desire.

What does it feel like to even contemplate the desires of your heart and your guts?

Invitation 11: A Story

Ignatius, our dear Iñigo, invited people to stories through the Exercises, and he invited people to put themselves in the stories, in this character or that character, maybe even as an onlooker watching the dynamics of a story unfold. It might be helpful to read this story that continues through the next many Invitations in the way Iñigo invited his retreatants in the Exercises to do so . . . slowly, imaginatively, pausing when we need to stop and consider something. Maybe we can even imagine ourselves as a character in the story. Maybe even take turns reading the story out loud to one another if you have the luxury of a companion traveling with you for this invitation.

Be prepared that this ancient story — modernized here — might be offensive to you at times, maybe even shocking. Such is the invitation to Wisdom . . . Sophia. It is a story that can be found in just about every tradition, a story of Wisdom making its way through the world and through us, our very flesh.

To get a glimpse of Sophia's clothes — let alone her eyes, her heart, her smile — we sometimes have to travel to the edges of life . . .

Let the images wash over you and see what comes for you . . .

You have this neighbor. Pathetic woman. She has been sick for years. Her doctors don't know what has been happening with her. She bleeds. For twelve years this has been happening. Yeah, the doctors don't know why, but people in your neighborhood have their own opinions. People talk. You hardly ever see her outside. She must sleep all day. What kind of energy would you have if you lost so much blood, not just a few days of every month but every day?! The doctors have not been able to help her — and she has been to many doctors. What's worse, she has spent nearly everything she owns on these doctors' bills. You heard she even had to take a second mortgage on her house. Probably on the dole, too. Her family has been unable, maybe unwilling to help. Well, there is her boy, but there's only so much a twelve-year-old can do. He's about all you see of both of them. Cuts the grass, takes out the garbage, walks to school. She's too weak for all that. When you do see her on that rare occasion — no matter the season of the year — she looks fragile, pale. You want to help her and her boy, you want to reach out — but something holds you back. When you do see her, after you get past staring for as long as she doesn't notice, just when she turns to meet your eyes, something in you walks the other direction, acts like you didn't see her, like you are busy.

Maybe you are kind of grossed out by her illness. There are stains on her hands, stains from the blood that trickles out of her, blood way more than any menstrual flow you have heard of. You think you see the shadowy stains even from a distance. Disgusting. If only she would wash her hands more carefully, at least get rid of the stains, something. Anything. Gloves, maybe? You feel sorry for her, for her boy, but if the doctors can't help her, what do you think you can do? You pray for her — when you think of it. You hear from some neighbors that she is addicted to drugs, painkillers you figure. Probably slept around way too much when she was younger. Maybe that's why she has this strange flow. That's probably it. Ruining that boy's life with her addictions. I bet he gets bullied at school. Poor boy. She can't even take care of herself, how can she take care of him?

But something very strange happened today. You were coming out of the grocery when you saw your neighbor in the parking lot down below the big railing. It looked like she was waiting for someone. You so rarely see her out. Probably buying alcohol to mix with her "prescription medications." You follow her eyes, try to see what she is looking at. There's a crowd that seems to have taken over part of the parking lot, a man in the middle, darker-skinned than many who might usually shop here. His clothes are rather scraggly, his hair not combed today. Another man in a suit has him by the arm and as he turns you see his face. Ah, the pastor from one of the churches a few neighborhoods away from this grocery. You've seen him interviewed on the news about the violence. On social media, you heard such sad news about his young niece. Very ill recently. Cancer. Not much time. Tragic. A large crowd — thirty, forty people? — has gathered around these two men down below the grocery store railing, the pastor seems to be trying to get this scraggly man moving. Maybe some of the crowd are with the scraggly man, his friends or something. They seem to be trying to keep people away, but it's useless. You wonder what this is about. Has he done something wrong? You don't see any police nearby, at least not yet.

Out of the corner of your eye, you see your neighbor begin making her way toward the crowd. The crowd must not know her, must not know her story, otherwise they probably would have gotten out of her way. You remember her hands — how filthy you imagine them to be — and something in you wants to warn them, but how can they hear you over this swelling mass of people? There's no one there you really know all that personally. You watch her, fearful of what she will do, she starts sliding between people. You feel sorry for them. They don't even know what she is doing, probably don't even know about her filthiness, the blood on her hands from that constant flow.

She sneaks in behind the scraggly man. You watch her carefully. What does she think she's doing?

She is jostled by the crowd. She gets separated from the guy for a moment, then reaches in one more time, grabs his shirt and then loses it again. Wait. What was that? Something happened. He stopped, looked around. What was that? No one else seemed to have noticed. You watch his lips, you try to make sense of his muttering. He asks some of the other people around him, "Who touched me? Who touched my clothes?" They must be his friends — they laugh at him. You hear them saying, "You see this crowd pushing and shoving around you and you ask, 'Who touched me?' Come on, man! Everyone is touching you, me, everyone. It's a mob here with this pastor — especially with everything that has been going on in this town!"

The pastor seems in a hurry to get him moving, but this guy stops, waits. He looks around him. You lean in closer, wonder what he's going to do. Is he mad? Will he lash out at her? Maybe he smells her, the blood. She doesn't smell good, you know that from living next to her. Her garbage cans.

He seems to have sized up everyone around him, then he sees her. Is she on her knees? What is she about to do? Maybe your neighbors are right about her, uh, her perversion. Good God, right out here in the open too! You can barely see her, she is nearly swallowed by the crowd. He takes her by that filthy hand and lifts her to her feet. He must not have looked closely at her hand. Well, he seems not so clean either. You look at her. Something seems different about her. She's shaking, trembling. You think she must be afraid, but that doesn't seem right. She looks, well, better in some way. Healthier than you have ever seen her anyway. There is color in her cheeks, a spark of life in her eyes.

You put your groceries down so you can lean in further to hear this. "I'm sorry," she says. "I'm sorry. I just knew that you could help me. But I didn't know how to stop you, talk with you. I, I touched your shirt, and, you see, I've had this problem for twelve years. I bleed—um—well—uh, way more than I should. And now, it seems to—I feel, uh, I feel better than I have in twelve years—"

The scraggly man cuts her off. You can barely make out the words. "It was (indecipherable) that healed you—" You try to make out what came next, but it's too loud, the shouting now picking up. He smiled at her. You wish you had caught everything he had said before. Despite his messy appearance, there is something about him. Like he knows something. Those eyes of his, goodness, like some deep light in them. You can't believe a man with such dirty clothes would stop you in your tracks. But those eyes of his. Wait, what's this? Oh my God, he kissed her hand, the inside of her dirty hand. That nasty hand! He'll probably get what she has, whatever it is. Hepatitis? Maybe worse. HIV? Ebola? Something terrible.

With that, the pastor pulls him away, the crowd following tightly, jostling them both around. Your neighbor is left behind. You don't know what to think about all of this. You still cannot believe he kissed that hand. Ugh! She had even told him about her problem.

You pick up your groceries and start making your way toward her. You would so love to go talk with her — what would you say? chide her for her brazenness? try to get a better glimpse of her seemingly better health? — but you haven't talked with her since she moved into the neighborhood. You say hello to her boy, that's about it. You feel sorry for him, not for his mother. And now you don't know what to think of her, of any of this.

You make your way home and have to think about all of this, what it all means.

Invitation 12: Conversing with a Wisdom Teacher

Let the story continue to unfold . . .

It was hard to sleep. Too much to think about. And then there were your dreams — those strange, disgusting events of yesterday. What was it that happened?

You look out the window. My God, there she is. In the yard! She is never there! Why, she's helping the boy pull those weeds! At least they're finally getting to that. But SHE's helping him. What happened yesterday? One minute she's touching that man, the next minute she looks, well, different.

You need to go back to the grocery — forgot the milk. How am I going to do this?, you wonder. You can't exactly say hello after twelve years of, well, basically ignoring her. Maybe just a quick wave, like that's what you've done for twelve years of being neighbors. You make it all happen quickly, like you're in a hurry.

Good God, what's going on at the grocery? Not a single place to park. You park across the street. "He healed that little girl, you know, the one with cancer!" Everyone was saying it, pointing at him. "On her deathbed yesterday and now she's up and walking around!" You follow their fingers, can't see what it is they are talking about. You make your way through the crowd and wonder what this is all about. Two days in a row at the grocery, and very strange things both days.

You see that man from yesterday. People are trying to get to him, but some of that scraggly crowd around him yesterday are pushing people out of the way. I guess those guys are his friends, you figure. They are as much of a mess as he is.

You try to get a little closer, to figure out why people are crowding around him. You shudder when you remember how he kissed her hand. He doesn't look sick yet. Yet. You hear it again: "That's him! That's the guy who healed the pastor's niece!" They are pointing at him. My God. What is this?

Out of the corner of your eye, you see them. They are rushing forward, trying to get past the, what are they, these well-worn thugs he seems to travel with? Bodyguards? They all shout at each other. You can't believe they are here! You feel your guts churn at your utter distaste for these people rushing in upon the guy who kissed your neighbor's hand. Where are these, uh, people coming from? They're going to ruin the neighborhood. The bodyguards push them away. The scraggly man swivels around, sees what is happening. He must be relieved that *he doesn't have to deal with them. Wait, what's he doing? He gets up and moves toward them. "Lay off them!" he screams. Is he yelling at them or at his bodyguards? "Wait! Get your hands off them! Let the *__________ through. Don't try to stop them!" The bodyguards can't believe it either. The *__________ rush through. They all grab the man. My God, he doesn't react. He lets them! There is a hush over the crowd. You can hear him speaking. "After all, the whole universe belongs to people like these. If you want to know what the heart of life is like, then you better be like these good people."*

What? What was that? Did he call these people good? Something in you knows you must leave. "What did I come here for anyway?" you wonder as you get your bearings. You make your way away from this madness and into the grocery store. You are in a daze. Did he really say that? And what about what they were saying about him, how he cured that little girl? On her deathbed, you had heard for sure last week. This is all too much.

*You pay for the milk and begin making your way around the crowd toward your car. Other people must have reacted like you did at what he said, at whom he got so close to — the crowds have thinned out. A small group of them are sitting down in the small shade of the parking lot, up by the berm. The bodyguards are there too, and some of the *__________ from earlier. How disgusting they are here. A few others too. Oh no, he's eating with them. He probably didn't even wash his hands after touching them. Ugh! You shudder to think what is probably building in his immune system — some terrible disease.*

You walk by. You try to not notice it all happening, try not to make eye contact with any of them. You wish you didn't have to walk this way, but you're already here. You hear voices, the sounds of eating. And then, from the voice of that man, "You want to know what the very heart of the universe — what some of you call God — is like? Well, it's like a little boy with diarrhea in a freshly filled pool." He laughs, a few of the others do too. How dare he insult God that way! To think that the pastor hung out with this man! You are so glad to be out of there. Just a few more steps and you'll never have to deal with this madness again. Surely they'll get cleared out of here before long. You think about calling the police yourself when you get home. You can't believe the pastor was hanging out with this man!

You slam the car door and sit there in the peace and quiet, alone, the shock of what you have witnessed the past two days completely overwhelming your every sense.

*_______ = you fill in the blank with some group of people you can barely even imagine would be human in our day

Perhaps, take some time to contemplate and journal about these questions:

What would be your reaction to all of these weird events in your neighborhood? What completely-off-the-social-map group of people would you put as the *________'s of the story? Why? What does it do to your body, your mind to even think about the possibility that these social rejects might have something to do with the heart of life? What would be your reaction to his likening the Universe, the very reality of God, to so-called people like this, to a boy with diarrhea in a pool?

Would you want to spend time with this man who seems to choose to hang out with — even eat with — the social rejects of the day, this man who touches and even kisses the filthy hand of your neighbor?

Is there anything about this man that intrigues you, that messes with your curiosity, your imagination, that disrupts your way of imagining?

Invitation 13: The Story Continues . . .

You get home from the grocery store. She waves to you like a long-lost neighbor. You wonder if she has washed her hands and wave back. At least if you had to shake her hand, she has those gardening gloves on now.

You stare at her in amazement. How did that happen with her? Twelve years of illness and moping around the house and then all of a sudden she's up and about like it never happened.

It all begins to make you mad, though you're not exactly sure why. Something about fairness maybe . . . how is it that she is healed, that this once-deathly-ill little girl everyone was talking about is apparently healed, but so many still suffer. You think about how you have suffered in life, the many ways you have hurt and still hurt . . . physically, emotionally, spiritually, socially. It seems your whole life has been one of hurt.

*You feel exhausted from thinking about all of this, maybe because you didn't sleep all that well last night. You try to take a nap on the couch, but all you can do is think about the strangeness of it all, of this man, of what he has said and done in that parking lot. How many times have you been there to shop and same old, same old. And now, he has the nerve to kiss a dirty and ill woman's hand and she is better, he apparently cures a little girl on her death bed, he embraces these *_______, and not only that, he eats with them and says they are to be imitated to know the heart of life. And then there was that ridiculous "diarrhea-boy in the pool" example. Who does this guy think he is? Everything you have witnessed is pretty bold. No matter how many times you let it all circle around your imagination, none of it makes any sense. You can't get the image out of your mind of him kissing her hand, of him accepting these *_______ into his presence, his embrace even. As much as it bothers you, you notice the gentleness, the tenderness of this man. Maybe you long for a tenderness like that, a gentleness with your own self that you have desired for much of your life. You wonder what it would be like to be with that group, to eat with them. What kinds of things do they talk about? You shake your head about even considering such a thing — such a strange group of people.*

While you are intrigued, it all continues to make you angry, that someone would be this way, in your neighborhood. Everything seemed so simple before this. There were the people who counted, people that mattered and those who didn't. There were the sick and the well. Things are becoming fuzzier and fuzzier in your mind.

Something in you begins to relax and before you know it, you are asleep. (Consider pausing here for a few minutes to simply be in the quiet for awhile . . .)

You awaken. Dreams have stirred even more in you. You wonder how long you have been asleep. The anger has cooled within you. Something in you wants to hear more from him; another part wants to confront him, call the cops on him, chase him out of town. You wonder if you can go back to the grocery, act like you are shopping again, listen a bit more.

You decide to go, another quick wave to the neighbor. She's still at it — her house finally looks decent. You had always wanted to pull those hideous weeds in front of her house. She was bringing down the property values for crying out loud. At least you don't have to worry about that anymore, you guess.

You pull into the parking lot, up near where they were earlier. Yep, they are still there, some of them anyway. You turn off the engine and try to listen to what they are saying. You thought you were close enough, but can only hear a few words every now and then. You wonder how close you can get without them seeing you. You put up your windows. It feels like you are gathering courage somehow, why you are not sure. They won't see you. There are probably hundreds of people who have passed by the last few hours.

With a deep breath, you get out of your car and hunker down behind the level of the next car so you won't be seen. You listen again, still unable to hear as much as you would like. You keep low and scoot around one car and then another, trying to get as close as possible. Ah, that's better. You can make out his voice, the one from when he was talking with those rejects earlier. What's he saying now?

Oh, another weird story. "You would think it would be that way, but is it? How about this . . . ? Two people went into the church to pray, one a Sunday school teacher and the other a politician. The Sunday school teacher is kneeling in the aisle right in front of the altar with his arms outstretched and a smug smile on his face. The politician enters and tries to get around him, but the teacher's books on fasting and penance are scattered all over the floor. The Sunday school teacher sneers at the politician when the politician accidentally steps on one of the books. The politician goes and sits in the last row, tries to get out of the way. He looks down at the ground, appears to be lost in thought. And all of a sudden, he puts his hands in his face and begins weeping."

"Nuh-uh. Politicians don't weep — and not in churches, for crying out loud!" "And what do they feel anyway? The things they say and do!" You can hear the people in the group are laughing at him, mocking him even. You look out through the car windows. His friends are laughing too, but they seem used to his weird stories. There's more talk, something about how politicians are among the most wealthy in the country, what do they know about our lives, on and on and on.

"That all could be true, but notice the way life is with these politicians and with all of us . . . the sun rises on both the bad and the good, and rain falls on both the just and the unjust."

How ridiculous! You laugh at this, but you notice that many in the group are thinking about it. You wonder how God could accept any of these people here, maybe even any of the politicians too. Just what is acceptable to God? What do you care? You have your own ideas about God and church — and they never seem to match what the pastor is saying — let alone what this crazy guy in the grocery store parking lot has to say.

Before you know it, that man is standing there a few feet from you. Oh no, how did this happen? You feel the grip in your stomach, terrified at being found out. "Hi there." He has squatted down a bit, his eyes at about the same height as you sitting there. He's just a few feet away. The first thing you notice is his smell, something like terrible body odor and the earth. You wonder when the last time was that he bathed. His shirt — the same one he had on the first time you saw him — has one of those knock-off designer insignias you see sold at the grocery store. It is filthy. "Hi," he says so simply. "What's your name?" You sputter it out and listen for his, though you are still so caught off guard that you can't even manage these exchanges demanded by the culture. "Would you like to come sit with us awhile? We're just talking. We have some food to eat if you're hungry."

He holds out his hand to you, that hand made dirty by touching all those people and whatever else. Who knows where else it has been? You would bet that he hasn't washed it since touching her—

But those eyes. No matter how dirty his body or clothes, something in those eyes seems so right, so good. Before you can even think about what you are doing, your hand is in his. You marvel at the touch of his hand . . . the warmth, the grittiness, you can't quite place the feeling you have touching him. You make sure to remind yourself to wash them before you get in your car. Another stop in the grocery.

*You untangle your legs and stand and before you know it he has introduced you to the group. They all seem friendly enough, but you find yourself still guarded around them. They make a space for you. You are both excited to be here and repulsed. You try to avoid contact with them as much as possible. After all, some of them are *_______, the ones you saw earlier. They get back to talking about politicians and church-types and the like. Every now and then, that man looks over at you. He seems to be checking on you. You try to act nonchalant, but everything overwhelms you. You wonder what it is you should do here, how you should act. You've never been in a situation like this. But you sit back and try to relax, try to take in the conversation. After all, this is what got you here in the first place.*

Invitation 14: Home and Back Again

After some time sitting there, you went home last night. Back to your house. Back to your house next to the neighbor who apparently was healed by him. You make a note to ask him about that, though you are still terrified to say anything in that group. But you listen carefully. They are all speaking your language, though you seem to have a difficult time understanding them. You're not sure why.

You've had a hard time sleeping the past two nights. Different reasons, though. Two nights ago there were things you couldn't get out of your mind. Now there's an excitement in you that you have not known for a long time.

How embarrassing that he found you hiding behind the car! But how glad you are. What is it about all of this that keeps turning over and over in your mind?

*You wonder where it is they slept last night. You left after a few hours of sitting there, when things seemed to be breaking up. The *______ were leaving, and it seemed right for you to leave too. Though you are still suspicious of them, you notice that they aren't a whole lot different from you. Strange the events of these past few days! What you find really bizarre is that they seemed to laugh at the same things you thought were funny, and they seemed thoughtful about things just as you did.*

You decide to go out to talk with them again. You make your way there, park your car again in about the same spot. Though you know you can't hide again behind the cars, you wonder if you can just waltz up to the group and sit down where you were yesterday afternoon. You decide to walk slowly toward the group and see what happens. For crying out loud, this is like high school all over again. You feel the butterflies in your stomach going a little crazy. How you hope they will—

"Hey! Come on over, we have your spot all warmed up for you!" One of the guys makes room for you. One of the women scoots over too and gives you something to sit on. It's cardboard, but it helps. You make quick eye contact with that man, and he acknowledges you, even says your name with a little smile. And there are those eyes again, how they blaze out of that dirty face, that mop of wild hair. You find yourself much more at ease than when you got out of the car.

The conversation continues, food is being passed around the group. You didn't eat anything yesterday, but decide to eat something small, something pre-wrapped. They all seem so kind, what could be bad here?

"But that guy — have you seen what he does?" One of the people he travels with is still ranting about the politician from yesterday. You can't remember if you voted for this one or not. He lists on and on and on all the terrible things this politician has done while in office, and his infidelities to the party and his many wives, his children from three marriages. He is very impassioned. That man with the eyes just sits there calmly and listens, giggles with the rest and shakes his head like the rest. You aren't sure if he's laughing at the way this guy is making his case or at the politician. There is a lull and the case-maker is catching his breath and seems to be hoping someone else will pick up for him. And then a voice, the one that you've really come to listen to:

"That all might be the case, friend. Yep, that all might be so. But how is it that you see the little speck in this senator's eye when you overlook the log stuck in your own?" He began looking around the circle for something. He grabbed a piece of mulch on the ground and then someone's walking stick. He threw the mulch to the guy who just offered the harangue and began walking toward him with the walking stick coming out of his own eye. "Hello there, Bob. I notice you have a little splinter in your eye. Well, I'd like to try to help you fix that." He kept trying to find a way to maneuver himself closer to Bob, much to the amusement of the group. "I can't quite seem to get there. Not sure what's blocking my way. But I see you are messed up and I want to help! I mean look at you!" Everyone was laughing hysterically, and so was Bob. He threw the mulch at him in jest. He continued with the act a few seconds longer before he sat down. How clever this guy is . . .

Consider taking a walk today to reflect on this story, maybe even on the times when you have found yourself having all the answers to make so-and-so's life perfect but have forgotten to work with your own problems and weaknesses and insecurities. Be gentle with yourself. See if you can laugh at yourself, at the times when you have done just what Bob did. If journaling is helpful, go with it.

Invitation 15: Considering Forgiveness

The story continues briefly . . .

The scraggly man says quietly, "We all mess up. That's the way life is, isn't it? Sometimes the mess ups are small and laughable, sometimes they are incredibly difficult, for us and for others. Forgiveness seems impossible. Maybe our prayer should be, 'let go and forgive what we owe just as we let go and forgive the ones who owe us.' What if that forgiveness flows through us only when we have unclenched our fists and our hearts about the ones who need our forgiveness? Sometimes that's easier to consider than other times, but it makes me wonder . . ."

*"Yeah, but have you seen what some of these people have done to us? Have you seen how they have treated us?" one of the *______ spoke up. You immediately feel guilt billowing out of the shadows within you. Perhaps you know exactly what that *_____ is talking about because you have done something like this to this person or to someone similar, one of the rejected ones of society.*

"No doubt, horrible things have been done to you. Test out the wisdom and see if it works. Only you can say. And maybe begin with someone who has wronged you not quite as much as these. Know that it doesn't mean you need to be best friends, know that this letting go a bit does not mean you agree with what this person has done to you. It just means you're letting a little breeze pass through your fisted hand and the experience you've probably been holding onto for some time. We all have moments of pain like this, no doubt. Just see if your hold on those painful experiences might be let go of just a little bit . . . the experiences will always be with us, they are a part of the fabric of who we are, part of that every-moment of our past that us brought us to this present moment. What happens in our lives when we let go of holding on so tight to any experience, even moments of grief and terrible pain? Just test out the wisdom, don't take my word for it just because I said it. What do I know? You're the Knower!"

Maybe spend some time journaling in the quiet about anything that this part of the story invites you to consider, or anything else from earlier in the story. Is such a forgiveness possible? Is it possible to let go of our hold on the past, to let go of our grip on the wrongs that might still be with us from long ago? Is it possible to live beyond them?

Invitation 16: An Ease . . . A Disruption

You wake up in your bed again to the light breaking through and the morning breezes making your curtains dance. Life is beginning to look differently for you. You seem happier in some way, like some light has been turned on from within.

You make your way toward the parking lot again. You find your spot, exchange greetings with everyone. There is an ease growing in all of this. There are a few new people here this morning, you make the point to smile at them, to make them feel welcome here as you have been welcomed these past few days. You're not sure you've ever seen them before. Judging by their clothes, they are probably not as well to do as you are. They are scruffy, maybe a little dirty, but they seem happy, like it's not a big deal to them.

He's speaking. It's pretty rare he gives speeches, but he seems in rare form.

"... do not worry about your life, what you are eating, what you are drinking, and not about your body — what you are wearing. Isn't your life much more than food and the body much more than clothes? Watch for awhile the birds of the sky, how they don't plant seeds, they don't harvest, they don't gather into barns for storage ... and yet Someone gives them food ... aren't you worth more than they are?! How from your worrying can you add one forearm's length to the height and breadth of your life? And why worry about your clothes? Learn something from the flowers of the field — how do they grow? They don't struggle or work hard or spin thread for clothes. And I say to you that not even the famously rich and beautiful King Solomon in all his radiant-beauty was clothed like one of these! If Someone dresses up the field-grass in this way — field-grass which lives today and tomorrow is thrown into the burning-oven — aren't you better than them, you who trust so little?"

He was on fire, that's for sure. But wasn't his logic going to burn him up? You know that you have to work hard to have a home like you do, a car, all kinds of things to wear and be proud of. This—

"Are all the celebrities on all the check-out magazines in there—" he said as he thumbed back at the grocery store behind him—"are any of them as beautiful as this chickory weed growing out of the sidewalk, even this dandelion over here that escaped the weed-killer? We'll be taken care of. Trust! That's the game, that's the invitation. And everything begins to work out. When we trust, we become aware of the ways of the universe. I mean, when you really think about

it . . ." He got up on his knees as if to proclaim something louder than just our group could hear.

"Congratulations, you beggars, you poor!
The whole Universe belongs to you!"

People in the circle were laughing, especially the poor. You aren't sure whether to laugh or hide. You are probably considered to be among the rich here, maybe just about anywhere. Your house, your car—all this talk today makes you uncomfortable. You begin to wonder what your neighbors would say about all of this. There were a few strange looks in the parking lot — people clearly uncomfortable by this group's growing presence here and the strange things that could be overheard. Your mind begins racing. A few days ago, you would have probably thought this guy was nuts, to be avoided. But he does have a point about those celebrities — they're not so hot underneath all that make-up. You've seen the internet photos of them — ugh. And they certainly seem just as messed up as anyone you know — the fourth-marriages, the abandoning of children, the addictions to this or that, the wasting of their wealth on ridiculous things. But congratulating the poor? What? Wouldn't that be the last group that would be congratulated? How can the poor own much of anything — let alone the entire universe?! How can that be? So many of them don't even go to church?! And what can they offer? You look across the circle at the raggedy clothes, at the —

You've worked hard for what you have. How dare he congratulate these slackers! What does trust have to do with any of this anyway? Anger begins building in you. You wonder what your place is here among this group.

One of the group speaks up. "Maybe you can tell us some stories. You know, like you have before. Help us all to understand a bit more."

"Great. Yes. How about this . . . the very reality of God is like a man who has terrible gas on an airplane."

People in the circle were laughing hysterically, but this is ridiculous!

"That's disgusting! It fills the entire cabin!" The words leap out of your mouth before you realize it. People in the circle are surprised, maybe even pleased to hear your voice. You realize that you might be the only person here in this group who has even been on a plane before, your head lowers in shame, embarrassment from speaking out.

"Yes. Exactly." He smiles at you. You realize you are on to something, but you're not yet sure what.

Consider creating your own short parables. Maybe as you go for a walk or as you stare out the window. Try using this formula to get on track . . .

the heart of the Universe **or** reality of God **or** kingdom of heaven **or** reign of God

is like

someone doing something crazy, ridiculous, negatively infectious, etc.

See if you can come up with anywhere between 5 - 10 parables. Talk with a companion to share ideas if that's helpful for you both.

What happens for you as you enter into this man's imagination?

Invitation 17: Take Nothing with You for the Journey!

You're not sure what to think about this guy and his crazy stories. But there is something about him that seems so good, like you want to trust him. You see your neighbor outside again. My God, she's planting flowers where the weeds once were. You laugh as you realize that her house will probably be the nicest looking on the block now. From eyesore to the new ideal. It's almost ridiculous.

You want to know about what happened to her. You've played that story through your mind so many times, and wished you could have caught what he said to her before he kissed her hand. Maybe you could ask her? How foolish. You remember that you have not ever really spoken with her — in your twelve years as neighbors! But the questions burn within you. Now that she's outside, you think, it's a lot easier to get to know her.

You gather the courage again. Open the door and walk outside. Before you know it, you are in her yard. You say hello, introduce yourself, say how glad you are to see her outside, try to make some excuse about how your schedules must never have matched up. She seems a little stunned that you are speaking to her, but she softens and accepts your invitation to getting to know one another finally. You say how good it is to see her so well. What beautiful flowers. She smiles. You tell her that you saw her at the grocery the other day, in the parking lot. "My God, you looked so sick, and then all of a sudden, you were better, I don't know ... like you are now."

She seems a little embarrassed by all of this. But she allows it, accepts where you must be going, does not shy away from it. "I happened to be above the railing and could see you in the middle of the crowd with him, and I noticed he said something to you — I couldn't make it out but I have to tell you that I was so intrigued with what happened, with the tender way he kissed your hand, how you seemed to be cured — I mean, look at you! I've been going to the parking lot every day since, to hear more of what he has to say." She seems amazed at this, didn't even know he was still in town. "Maybe this is a personal question, I'm sorry — but what made you go?" You two talk for some time, explaining your motives, what has called you to know more, understand more, to discover some sense of being whole through your participation. Finally you get the courage to ask what really got you here in the first place ..."Would you be willing to tell me what he said to you, you know, before he kissed your hand?" She seems embarrassed at this, like she wishes you hadn't asked this. "I'm sorry if I have offended you by asking, but, it's just that I'm so curious about this guy. Did you hear that he cured the pas-

tor's niece? She was on her deathbed! And then you, how he cured you from whatever you were suffering from..." You feel the pangs of guilt for doing nothing for this poor woman and her boy. "No, I hadn't heard that. That's really strange to me." She seems genuinely surprised at the news of the niece. "Why would you be surprised? I mean, clearly he has some special powers. He healed you. I saw it with my own eyes! Right there in the parking lot." She looks down, almost like she didn't want to have to remember all that. Something seemed rather strange about all of this to you.

You decide that you had better go — you've stirred up enough here after being so absent for twelve years. What a neighbor you have been — and then to come over here with a million questions! You try to be as gracious as possible as you back away, though you wished you had gotten the information about what he said to her, what really got you to walk over here. Just as you turn to leave, she says something strange. "He said, 'I didn't do anything. It was your trust that healed you.'" You turn around, surprised at what she said. "And then he kissed my hand." She holds it up, you notice that it looks like anyone's hand, though a little dirty with soil from the flowers. You think about this for a moment, realize what had really happened. Was this even possible? You smile, and thank her, turn your body toward her for the first time maybe, reach out for her dirty hand even and shake it between both of your hands, and leave.

You are in your car before you realize it, and have parked and are out of the car like you are on some kind of mission. You know what you want to say to him, how strange all of this is. How it doesn't add up — the pastor's niece he supposedly healed, brought her back from the dead practically and then your neighbor whom he supposedly didn't even help but told her she had healed herself with her . . . gulp . . . "trust". He's sitting there speaking again, and although you don't have the patience to sit down, you notice there seems to be some urgency to his words.

"Well, he'll be back in a few minutes, I'm sure. Probably with police even. But maybe there's an opportunity here. After all, all of the greats were wanderers as well, so no need to feel so tied down here to this particular place. We've only been here a few days anyway, and it has served us well. And best for us all to split up for awhile anyway, huh? Time for us to head out in pairs, set the world on fire in our own ways and find out how all of this works. You know, see what you can do, see what can be born through you. Take nothing with you for the journey — no extra clothes, no wallet or purse. Just go with what you're wearing. Trust that you'll be taken care of, and eat whatever is put before you. Heal the sick. Announce to everyone that now is the time to realize what we are all made of, *that the heart of the Universe can be found in the here and now, so close you can grab it. We'll meet back here in a few days and then make our way together to wherever the wind carries us next."*

"Hey, we've seen you do these things, we saw you cure that little girl, but what's to think WE can do that?" a man said as he looked at his hands befuddled.

Another voice from the group, "And how are we to know we'll be safe? How are we to know we'll get what we need? I mean, we're not flowers and we're not birds!"

The man we had all been gathering around giggled, seemed surprised anyone remembered what he had said about flowers and birds from a few days ago. "Rest easy, friends. We can all do this. Just get moving, and discover for yourselves. There's nothing so special about me . . . you too will be taken care of. I mean really, ask for what you really, really need — and you're going to get it. Get in touch with your heart's deepest desire — and you will find it happening right before your eyes. Knock at any door where your heart leaps up within you — and trust that that door will swing wide open for you. This is what trust is all about, right? Now go find out for yourselves!"

"But what about you? Who gets to be your companion? I want first dibs!" Immediately people from the group were elbowing their way closer to the man. You couldn't believe how relaxed everyone was the past few days, and now there was chaos.

"I'm staying here. I'll just get in the way of your discovering that it all flows through you when you allow it, give it permission. I'll see you in a few days, and we'll have all kinds of stories to share with one another about adventures." He looked over toward the grocery store entrance where a few police cars had pulled up. The officers were getting out of their cars and talking with the store manager. "Thinking you better be off. Find a friend and go!" he smiled at everyone. As they were leaving, he called after them to encourage them, "Trust! Your adventures will be great ones!"

There he stood all alone. You had forgotten what had led you here so fast in the first place. You wondered where he would stay, where he would go. You look into his eyes — they always looked so deep, so full. "Where will you go?" you ask.

"Oh, I'm not sure."

"Where have you been staying?"

He pointed to some of the cardboard left behind. "Birds have nests, and animals have lairs and homes, but humanity's child has nowhere to rest." He smiled.

The words leap out of your mouth before you realize it. "Would you like to stay at my place?" He smiles at your invitation, his eyes recognizing the opportunity. "Yes, sure. That would be nice. Thank you."

You show him your car, and both get in and head to your house. Your neighbor's flowers look very nice, and you think about inviting her over later to meet him, well, to get to know him. You show him your house and immediately notice how shabby he looks against your home, your possessions. What will this time with him be like?

Maybe take some time to journal about any questions you might ask this wisdom-teacher, things that have been on your mind recently or for some time.

Invitation 18: In Your Home

Well, here he is at your dinner table. Maybe you invite others to join you, maybe you'd rather it be a one-on-one conversation. You begin to ask him any questions you have.

Eventually, he says, "Hey, what you pile up in your treasure-chest is there in your heart too, you know?"

You ask him, "And what do you value, what's your treasure?" You look at his clothes, apparently all that he possesses.

"Wisdom," he smiles.

"And how do you get that?" you ask. Perfect, this is what you've wanted to know all along.

"You've probably heard the poem before, right? Wisdom, Sophia, says,

I love my lovers! My seekers find me!
Rich and distinguished are they who are with me!
What's valuable grows . . . honesty . . . the truest of intentions!
My fruit is better than gold — the finest gold!

"Such is the way of Wisdom, right? When you have a little bit of wisdom, it grows and multiples once you start using it. You grow to be clever, you can see underneath the surfaces of things. And, unlike, gold, no one can steal Wisdom from you. It is the truest wealth.

"And she, Wisdom, goes on to say something to the effect that she is older than the hills, she was there at the creation of the world. Whomever finds her finds life. Whomever passes by her finds death and destruction. You see, Wisdom has built her house, and that house might be larger than you and I can imagine — larger than the container of the earth itself, huh? Yes, Wisdom has built her house, and all we need to do is enter."

"But how? Where is this house? Where must I go?" You immediately feel like you should have been on the adventure with the others, on foot over all the earth instead of tied down in this house of yours. Maybe then you would know this Wisdom.

He continues, "Wisdom has built her house, she has put a wonderful banquet together and invites all to taste of it. How do you get to the house, how do you eat of the banquet? Memorizing the wisdom of the ancient-ones? Maybe there's another way. Maybe it's all easier than that, and yet infinitely more challenging. Maybe if you want to be as wise as the ancient-ones you must do as they did . . . ."

"And what is that?" the words fly out of your mouth, like an animal on the prowl.

"Well, try looking within. Try dawdling along through a day or two and see what you discover in the quiet. I'll join you in it, and then we can see what we discover. Such are the ways of the wise ones, those who reflect on their experience and find the gold within."

Consider taking a day or a weekend to simply be in the quiet, to dawdle as this wisdom-teacher invites. What happens within us as we rest in the quiet, as hard as it might be for the first hour or so?

Again, if you feel like you need to talk with someone, feel free . . . a companion, a professional if the need should arise, a neighbor.

To Wisdom's House . . . Dear Sophia!

Maybe go for a slow walk. What is it you would like to know, to discover in the quiet? You might consider holding a specific intention in the quiet, or perhaps just let whatever needs to come to you come . . . .

If you are trying this invitation among others in the quiet, perhaps consider even eating your meals together in the quiet. Is it possible to know their desires for life and for love, to know them even more intimately in the quiet?

Do what you know in your heart you need to do now . . . a contemplative walk, yoga practice, draw, journal, paint, find a quiet place to sit. Give yourself permission to learn how to be lazy.

When was the last time you rested on the earth, looked up under the canopy of a large tree and watched the light dance around you from under the leaves?

When was the last time you watched the sun slip down over the edge of the horizon into who-knows-where?

When was the last time you gazed at the moon, at its loveliness, watched the stars move through the sky so slowly?

Take some time to rest here awhile . . .

Invitation 19: Dancing with Sophia?

As you rest in the silence for some time, maybe even consider setting a chair next to the threshold, the doorway of a room that has some open space in it.

Rest in the chair for some time as you gaze into the open room before you, as you rest here on the threshold.

Do you have a lived awareness of the immense water that makes up your body? As you sit here, perhaps imagine your body is in a tank of water, a tank filled just to below your chin. It's easy to rest here awhile because the water is at a perfect temperature for you, and your face is safe above the brim of the water.

Can you feel the ripples the water makes outside you even when you are as still as possible, gentle ripples as your body moves to breathe, as your heart beats its perfect rhythm? If it feels good for you, see how gently you can increase the rippling of the water in the gentlest of ways as you simply feel the effects of your body in this water. What is this your body knows? What is this your body remembers?

What is this ocean within you?

Perhaps these ripples even begin to move you out of your chair, right in the doorway of the open room. Look at that wide, open space in which you can move easily, freely, a space where you don't need to worry about furniture being in your way.

As you feel this ocean continuing to surround you, perhaps it begins moving you over the threshold and into the room. Or if you're content to rest in your chair and imagine the dance through you, wonderful. In whatever way feels right for you, tune into the rhythm ... of your heartbeat, your breath, of music, maybe of the symphony of sound around you. Maybe the room has a particular energy or feel to it. Whatever it is you sense, consider moving gently and freely through this space ... dance, moving to no particular pattern but your own.

Let the dance be wild, seductive, funny, whatever you feel called to in this moment.

Luxuriate in the freedom of movement. Let there be no judgment to how or why you move in the way you do.

Such is the dance that so many have danced before us. Such is the dance of Sophia, of Wisdom in the Flesh.

Let it be all of you.

Invitation 20: Sharing the Journey in Wisdom's House

As you come to the end of your time in the quiet, consider finding a meaningful way to end this time. If you are with others, maybe gather again in the quiet for about thirty minutes before entering into conversation with one another, or maybe even make a meal together in the quiet and once the meal is ready and you are gathered at table, break the silence in any way that feels right for you.

What can be discovered when we sit at Wisdom's table, at the feast she has laid out there before us all?

Listen deeply to what your companions have to say too. What are you discovering together through these Exercises, through the quiet, through this life?

Invitation 21: The Story Continues . . .

You are back at your dining room table with the man from the supermarket, the wise man you have invited into your home. You share with each other the gifts you've found in the silence and the challenges. Sometimes you find such peace in the silence, other times it feels like so many voices are shouting at you in the silence, voices competing for your attention within.

"This might seem crazy," he says, "but make a list of all the qualities in others that really bother you. You might even hate these qualities, maybe even feel hate for people who exhibit these qualities. No worries — simply create your list and see what shows up there and briefly explain why each of these qualities bothers you so much. A list of at least ten qualities would be helpful."

Invitation 22: Once You Have Your List Ready . . .

With your list in hand, you sit with this new friend. You think back to the past few days with him, remember watching him as you both sat in the quiet, how he would be so still for so long. Sometimes, you found yourself antsy, having a difficult time of it all. Sometimes wonderful memories would spring forth from within. Other times, difficult moments would come forward. Sometimes you would think about people, why they bother you, what it is about them that sometimes makes you angry. You tell this new friend all this, pour your mind and heart out to him. He seems to sit there and listen without any judgment, even as you share your list of the qualities in others that you cannot stand, qualities that you might even hate. You might feel some embarrassment about each of these qualities, even a tinge of the hate within you.

Then he finally speaks up. "You know, we all have enemies. We all have people in our lives who push our buttons, who know just what to do to aggravate us. Sometimes they might have hurt us badly, maybe we've even hurt them. You know what I have found to be the most helpful in those moments? I try to love them, I try to love my enemies and when I have the time, I pray for them, meditate for them, send them love from a distance." He let it sit right there.

There's nothing you can do to hold it. The words erupt from your mouth. "What? Are you kidding? I HATE when they do these things. Sometimes I even hate them. How can I love them? That's crazy-talk."

He smiles again. "Yeah, I completely understand. But when people really bother me, sometimes even when they have done or said terrible things to me or about me, I find a quiet place and I think about them. I remember all the terrible things they have done or said. Sometimes I cry. Sometimes I get even madder. And then I breathe, find my center again, kind of like we did in the quiet the other day. And after I've calmed down, I begin to wonder about these people, my enemies. I wonder why they might have done that. I think about what they might have been feeling to have done these things. I wonder what life experiences might have led them to do these things. Were they ever tormented when they were kids or when they were adults that would make them act this way? And usually, a spring of compassion wells up inside of me. I begin to understand these people, I see the larger dynamic of why they have acted that way toward me. It doesn't make what they did to me right, but I begin to see it in different terms. It feels a bit easier, when I am ready, to offer them love, even from a distance, even if they are resting in the grave and we still walk the earth. Sometimes I even find myself getting a little more honest with myself and have to admit that I have done something similarly to someone else." He paused there, let the words hang in the air a bit between us.

"And in that honesty, I begin to notice that I hold power over others in my own unique ways. You know, treat them like they are somehow below me, that I am better than they are, more important, more valuable. Ever heard of mimesis? In psychology, mimesis is the understanding that we tend to mimic or copy or even embody the very things in others that we cannot stand, the qualities in others we even hate. Have you ever noticed a time when you might have said or done something to someone else that is very similar to the actions or words of others that you cannot stand?"

You think about this for some time. You have to be honest and you tell him what you think.

He smiles and continues gently, "So when we love our enemies, we really end up loving whom? Not only them but ourselves too. And who needs love more than ourselves? Most of us aren't always so good to ourselves. You know Gandhi, right? Here's a man who was clubbed repeatedly in South Africa for protesting early forms of apartheid, then he gets tossed out of the train because he was the wrong skin color for that compartment. Then all kinds of terrible things happen to him in India, including many jailings, etc. And you know what he advocates? Recognizing our own imperfections, loving our enemies.

"Look at the pedestals we place under our leaders, and how sad we are to see them fall from such grace and respect. Why do we expect perfection from them when we have so much trouble getting it right ourselves? When will we finally realize we are all human, all perfect in our own way and yet not yet finished? When will we realize that people see both the goodness in us and the parts that are still waiting to be healed, waiting to be found in their own wholeness?

"So what would your life look like if you loved yourself as you are? What would you life look like if you trusted your own goodness, even in the midst of all the little things that bother you about yourself? What would your own life look like if you loved your enemies? What would it look like if you indeed, in your own way, offered them love and at the same time loved the goodness of your own self?"

Invitation 23: A Meditation

Maybe sit back awhile and rest easy. Close your eyes or at least soften them . . .

As you take some time to relax, notice your left leg . . . your right leg . . . your left arm . . . your right arm . . . your torso . . . your head . . . this amazing body we have been given to live within for sometime. Take some time to feel whatever life you feel in your limbs, in your whole body.

When you are ready, bring to mind someone you love dearly. Of course, this person could be living or dead, just be sure it is someone you really love. Notice the person's eyes, their skin, the way their voice sounds, the ways they move and live. Maybe there's even a particular smell or taste you associate with them, some food you might have often enjoyed with one another. Take some time to enjoy being with this person. Feel the love you have for this person. Give yourself permission to feel the love this person has for you, and give yourself permission to feel in some way the love that exists between you and this person — no matter the distance between you and this person.

pause and be here as long as you need, as long as you like . . .

After finding some time for sharing love with this person you love dearly, maybe bring to mind someone that you know very little, someone in your life now or even someone on the other side of the planet. Imagine looking deeply into the person's eyes, listen for the sound of their voice, the way the light glimmers off their skin, notice the way this person moves and lives their life on this earth. Is it possible to tune into the beating heart within this person, the heart that beats out a rhythm that is very different from yours and yet that is syncopated at moments? Is it possible to notice that you are breathing the same air, eating food from the same earth — even half a world away? As you consider this person and wonder about this person, is it possible to feel any love for this person with whom you are sharing life on this planet, this person with whom you are journeying to who-knows-where with our lives, with our arising each morning and our surrendering to sleep and dreams every night?

pause and be here as long as you need, as long as you like . . .

And after considering this stranger, this person you do know personally all that well, maybe bring to mind someone who has aggravated you at times in your life, someone with whom you might not like to spend time or space, maybe even someone who embodies some of the qualities from your list . . . someone you can barely stand to be around. Perhaps imagine yourself observing this person from a distance without them noticing you . . . notice the way this person moves through life, notice how they breathe, how the light reflects off their skin, their face. Maybe even see if you can get a glimpse of this person's eyes. Take all the time you need here, and see if you can observe with as little judgment as possible . . . is it possible to offer this person love? Even though this person might have wronged us — even terribly, tragically — is it possible to feel any love for this person simply because this person is a human being just like you are, just like the other people are with whom we have shared this meditation? Is it possible to feel love moving out from you to this person? Or is it possible to notice that you and this person can exist in a sea of love, an ocean of love much larger than the both of you?

pause and be here as long as you need, as long as you like . . .

And when you are ready, very much taking your time, slowly come back to your own body, your own self resting here. Notice again your legs, your arms, your torso, your head . . . your whole self. What do you feel in your own body right now? In what ways do you feel the life — the immensity of this life — moving through you? Is it possible — with all the history we have with our own selves, all the qualities we know to be "good" and all the qualities that we are somehow ashamed of, maybe even embarrassed by? Is it possible that you can love yourself, that you can feel love for your own self right here and now? Is it possible that you can experience some love for yourself, you with all your own flaws? Is it possible to love someone who is not perfect?

pause and be here as long as you need, as long as you like . . .

Rest easy for awhile here. What does such love look like, feel like, sound like? Is it possible to notice that such a love as this surrounds us and moves within us and beyond us, even without our own doing? Is it possible that a love like this has a life of its own if we have the eyes to see, the ears to hear, the heart to understand?

pause and be here as long as you need, as long as you like . . . and when you are ready, take your time to come back to yourself in the here and now.

Consider journaling about your experience with this meditation, or maybe go out for a walk and reflect on your experience.

Invitation 24: An Old Way Brought Forward Again and Again and Again . . . for a New Future in this Profound Present

Let the story continue . . .

He asked me, "So, after having some time to think about it all, have you noticed any moments when you have said or done to someone else the very thing you hate in others?"

"Well, I have to admit there were a few moments where I caught myself doing that. But there are so many others where that didn't work, that mimesis theory. I mean, I don't do ***all*** *of those things on my list of qualities I can't stand in others!" He just smiles at you as you read through some of them. Compassion seemed to radiate from him, maybe a peace you wish you knew better, a peace you wish you could find within yourself more often. Even so, you might find yourself getting defensive. "And besides, what about all those people who hold me down, who have bullied me somehow, who have exerted power over me? What about them? I mean, I can offer them love upon love upon love, but sometimes I just feel like a doormat, like my attempts at love for them do not change anything!"*

"Ah, that's very good. How very good of you to bring that up. Well, it seems to me that there are some choices when people try to hold power over us . . . we could lash out at them in some way, physically or verbally or emotionally . . . but does that solve the situation? Nah, doesn't it usually seem to make things worse? And besides, doesn't that then mean that you are playing their game? That you are holding power over them, dominating them in some way? What are some other responses, huh? We could run away from them, avoid them, try not to think about them, right? But does that really solve it? Maybe for the time being, but every time you see that person, don't your bristles stiffen and you find yourself on edge? And doesn't that anxiety then ripple over into your other relationships? Or even every time the person comes to mind, you feel the rage simmering within you? Fight or flight — they don't seem to do it do they? Maybe there's another way, maybe other ways, to handle the situation. Let's say that you got into a some kind of accident with someone and they feel you are at fault, negligent, and they said they were going to sue you for everything you've got, you know the standard American line. What could you do?"

"I don't know. I guess hire a big-time, expensive lawyer!"

"Sure. Maybe you'd do that anyway. But why does someone do that? Why does someone 'sue you for everything you've got'?"

"Well, they probably want all my money to soothe their pain. But I think there's more to it than that. It seems like they are trying to get even, maybe even get one over on you, control you somehow."

"Yes. Say you are in the courtroom and that person's lawyer has made their case and it's your side's turn to speak. And you stand up and place your wallet on the table in front of you, your car keys, everything of value you have on you. You take off your expensive clothes you wore for the court proceeding, your shirt, you slip off your shoes. You begin reaching for your belt before someone asks what in the world you are doing. And you say, 'He said he wants everything I have, so I'm giving it to him.' And he chimes in, 'I don't want those,' he points to what's on the table, what's left on you. 'But these are very nice pants, and these socks are worth a couple bucks. You can have them both. Clean pair of underwear too, pretty new,' you say as you slip off each item of clothing, each possession. And what do you imagine he says?

"'Stop! I don't want those—'"

"And you respond? 'But you said you wanted everything. And here it is,' as you stand there completely naked in the courtroom. Sure, you're probably in contempt of court, but what have you exposed before the whole world?"

"Your naked self!"

"Yes, and what else besides this man's attempt to hold power over you. What's he going to see? Well, pretty quickly, he's going to see that you are human being just like he is, you're made of the same stuff as him. And when we see that, how quickly we have the opportunity to realize that there is indeed no reason to hold power over anyone. We're all human, we're all made of the same stuff, we're all children of this same world. The sunlight and the rain fall on each one of us, whether we are good or bad in each other's eyes." He let that sink in for awhile before he spoke up again. "Maybe you'd like a story I once heard . . . ?

A Story

How our parents let us go down there, all alone, before the world of cell-phones or the internet, amazes me.

We packed ourselves into a van, drove nearly twenty hours, and arrived in the Florida beach city at 4 AM. Interesting planning on our part, for sure.

We had only seen the place we were staying in a brochure. The lady sounded nice enough on the phone. And when we were led to our room, it ended up being about half the size of my bedroom at home. And there were seven of us.

What did it matter, we all thought, we're on Spring Break!

We headed to the beach right across the busy street from the hotel. While we were pretty early arriving at the beach, it didn't take us long to realize that there were more people here around our grandparents' age than our own. A few more high school groups, some college-aged students, hundreds of our grandparents, and us.

We found our silly ways to have fun on the sand, in the water. We were on Spring Break after all!

The sun set on our beach party, and we decided to head back to the room and get something to eat. And after all of that, we did what everyone our age did when the beach was quiet — cruise the main drag to see who might be interesting to us and our young hormones.

After awhile of walking up and down the sidewalk, we crashed on the hotel's pool-deck that was raised a few feet above the sidewalk of the main drag. We laughed and had a good time chatting with people who walked by. The retirees were long in bed, only the younger generations still out on the night-prowl.

All of the sudden, during a lull in the conversation, we heard a terrible crash in the distance, like glass being broken. We stood up to see what this was all about. Down the street, we saw a group of guys and girls laughing hysterically. One of the guys was pushing over the big flower pots that lined the street and sidewalks. He then picked up one of those coin-automated newspaper-stands chained to a No Parking sign and smashed it to the ground, the noise echoing all the way down to where we were by the pool deck. His friends thought he was hilarious. Without a word, we sized them up, realized they were a little older than us, bigger, stronger. And the way they were all walking and laughing, they had to be drunk, maybe high. We didn't say anything significant to one another there on the pool deck, but something in us knew what to do . . . to sit ourselves down and not draw any attention to ourselves as the drunken idiots walked our way. "Look away, act like you never saw anything, do nothing to draw attention to ourselves," the silent, instinctual code among us.

So we sat down and tried to not look at them when they passed by our area. But one of us must have made eye contact or something. "Hey, which one of you rich little faggots wants to fight me?" he said as his friends continued their hysterical laughing at his antics. "Come on, which of you faggots is it going to be?" We all froze, looked over his shoulder to hope we'd see a cop we could flag down. But nothing—

He continued his taunts as some of the girls with him joined in. One of my friends leaned into me and whispered, "I have a knife back in the room—"

"Jesus, you brought a knife with you on Spring Break—" He was about to get up, our friend who said he liked to fight in junior high with a bat at his side. I grabbed his arm and held him back, whispered to him to shut up and let this idiot get bored with us and pass us by.

Unfortunately, our drunk friend below us upped the ante. He took off his shirt, threw it to the ground, and flexed his biceps, his chest. He was ripped, strong, no match for any of us, maybe no match for three of us together. The girls with him pealed out their laughter. "Come on, who wants to take on one of these?" he said as he kissed his bicep.

It took everything I had to hold back my friend who indeed wanted to fight the idiot. I knew that if he fought the guy, we'd all get drawn in and the idiot's friends too. It didn't take a genius to figure out that someone was going to get hurt very badly. I pictured myself having to call my parents from the hospital, even worse from jail.

The idiot continued his taunts, and when none of us responded, he ran around to the open side of the deck and made his way up to our level. "Come on, faggot. Who's going to fight me?" he asked as he stood over us and pushed each one of us to try to incite some reaction. I was amazed my friend didn't react, incredibly grateful he was heeding my request that he not fight as I dug my fingernails into his forearm to hold him back. "Well, how about you? Huh?" The idiot focused his attention on the African-American guy from our group, called him some terrible names. All of our jaws dropped, even the idiot's friends down below on the sidewalk were surprised by the idiot's drunken bravado, foolishness. But that did not stop him despite the cool chill now in the air from his insults as he continued to push our friend around on this warm night. Our friend looked to be half his size — maybe. I couldn't believe he wasn't going crazy at what the idiot was saying — no matter the glaring size difference. But he just calmly looked into the idiot's eyes as he pushed him around in his chair. "Come on, faggot. Get up and fight!" he said as he stepped back and hurled even more insults at him. His friends laughed with him again, though a little uneasily. And that's when our friend looked deeply into the idiot's eyes and calmly stood up. The idiot and the friend I had been holding back both cheered. The idiot stepped back a step, kind of amazed. "Yeah! Finally one of you little rich faggots has some courage!" Our friend just stood there calmly, simply, no real challenge for this beast of a guy with his shirt off. His eyes soft, with a glimmer like he knew something that no one else there seemed to know, he stared even more deeply into the idiot's eyes. And then he reached out his hand into the space between the two of them — him and the idiot — and kept his eyes locked on the idiot's eyes. And with his hand open there in the space between them, our friend said very calmly, "My name is David. What's yours?"

The idiot took a step back, all befuddled all of the sudden. He stumbled over his feet a bit, the alcohol suddenly revealing how shallow he really was. "I, uh, I don't want to know your name, I, I just wanted to beat the crap out of ya." The chill in the air came to life again as he looked at his friends down below on the sidewalk. Even they were silent, unsure how to react. The idiot looked away from all of us, walked back in the direction from which he had come up on the deck and made his way back onto the sidewalk. He looked back at David for the briefest glance and then reached down to pick up his shirt before he walked off, his friends right behind him.

Invitation 25: Reflecting on Nonviolence . . . Jujitsu

He turns and asks, "What had David done here? When someone was trying to hold power over him, what had he done to invite a different way — a gently jarring way — to calmly invite the oppressor to wake up and realize what he is doing? How did simply standing up and telling him his name and asking for the other guy's name change everything?"

"I don't know. Maybe David woke him up somehow, made him realize what he was doing, if even for an instant."

"Yeah, I think so too. You see, if David had fought the guy, he would have found himself in a hospital. If he would have run off, maybe he could have gotten away from the situation, but how would David have faced future confrontations, especially when he had been so insulted before his very friends? Maybe sometimes the right thing to do is indeed to run, to avoid harm. But David took a risk. He stood up for himself, he stood his ground, and he, in a sense, held up a mirror to the bully to invite him to see for himself how ridiculously he was acting. And David had to do it out of love, he had to do it in such a way that showed that he was equal to this bully, no better and no worse. And such moments like this open up the possibility for transformation, for change . . . for all of us."

"But how did he know what to say? Do you think that before he left for Spring Break, he thought, 'Well, if anyone tries to push me around, I'll stick out my hand and introduce myself?' Probably not. The very nature of Wisdom, the very heart of nonviolence like this, is to trust that the right thing will be said, that the right thing to diffuse the situation will be spoken through you. The nature of Wisdom is to trust that you will get what you need. You're never standing there alone."

"But how do you account for people like Gandhi, Martin Luther King, so many more who were killed when they used nonviolence? I mean, isn't there a risk?"

"There certainly is a risk. A question I always ask myself is, of the options that present themselves in any situation of conflict, what choice invites the most life? Running away, fighting it out, or letting another possibility, a third way, to emerge?"

"But they died, every single one of them. King, Gandhi—"

"Like I said, there is a risk. But sometimes in running away from the problem, don't we cause more violence? In fighting it out, do we usually solve it, get to the

heart of the issue that created the problem in the first place? When we open ourselves to a third possibility, when we open ourselves to loving our enemies, something pretty incredible begins to happen within us, within the conflict, even within our oppressors. We can have courage that everything we need will come to us. So often it does. This whole life is a lot bigger than us, you know." He looked deeply into my eyes, like he knew something, saw something in me that I had shied away from most of my life. "It comes down to knowing who you are, right?"

"You mean like David, how he introduced himself to that idiot?"

"Uh, yeah, and more than that, I think. It's as if David knew something, didn't he, when he stood up, when he stretched out his hand, right?" He gave me some time to think about that.

"Isn't it amazing what can be accomplished when we engage Lady Wisdom, when we allow her to enter our world?

"How is it that Gandhi can inspire hundreds of men and women to peacefully march on the Dharasana Salt Works and allow themselves to be clubbed and stomped and beaten by the British police? Witnesses tell the story that it was at that moment that India showed that Britain could no longer govern them, indeed if they ever really had.

"How is it that Rosa Parks, tired of more than just the day's work, could finally say 'No!' and thus inspire an entire generation to choose another way?

"How is it that Martin Luther King, Jr., and the Montgomery Improvement Association could lead a bus boycott that ultimately raised the hopes and possibility of seeing that Jim Crow was no longer tenable in a 'free society' AND get nearly 100% full participation from the hordes of people who needed to get places, to work, to family, etc.?

"People rise up and work together, discover the truth together, when Wisdom is engaged and trusted. Superpowers can be toppled, unjust laws that we have lived with for generations without much questioning can be exposed and overturned, bullies wake up to their actions and discover the humanity of the victims of their anger, relationships of domination can become relationships of co-discovered equality.

"There are so many stories that could be told, so many more. Maybe you even know some that must be told. And they must be told — they give us courage, they give us possibilities. Now, of course, nonviolence has a price, a cost. The aggressor can get even madder and clobber, even kill you. There is a risk. And sadly, so many of our heroes have been killed at the hands of their aggressors . . . But when it comes down to it, don't we realize, don't we know in our own guts that nonviolence works, indeed it might be the only strategy that works in the long term?

"You see, if the Universe is indeed Infinite, then aren't we all part of something much greater than we usually realize? Maybe that's what we glimpse when we invite a new way — that there really is so little distance between each other. Maybe it's only in conflict that we discover it. Who knows? The Infinite includes everyone, all possibilities, right? But what do you do then with evil? Well, maybe evil must be called back to goodness, and what strategy to use better than non-violence? Those who try to exert power over us need to be called back to what we've all known all along, all the way back to our times on the playground . . . that we are all equals, that we are all made of the same stuff, that we are all children of God. And with that, what more can I say?

"Well, I have certainly enjoyed my time here with you, but now it's time for me to be moving along."

"No, you can't go. It seems like I was just beginning to get it."

"You're well on your way, always have been. Besides, there's nothing else I can do for you. It's time for you to figure things out on your own. Wisdom, Sophia has found you, and you have embraced her. You've got plenty to work with, and now it's time for you, time for everyone to begin bringing forward ever new invitations to Wisdom's banquet. What can you allow to be said through you that will wake up people to the goodness of life? What can you allow to be done through you, through your body, that can reveal to others the very heart of life, the heart of the universe? What dreams can be dreamt through you for a world ever new and renewed? What can you say or do to invite others into this inner knowledge that the very reality of God is ever present, that all we need to do is open our eyes to see, clean out our ears to hear, have the courage to open our hearts to understand? It's all within you . . ."

Invitation 26: Practice a Day of Mindful Ease

If it feels right, take some time to practice another day of mindful ease.

Consider just waking up when you wake up in bed — no alarm, no need to rush to the next event. Rest here awhile, let your nightdreams stir within you. No need to judge them, no need to do much of anything ... see if you can spend the day just letting everything be. Note what it feels like to be here in bed, snuggling up with yourself for a time.

When you finally feel it's right to get out of bed, let your day simply unfold. Consider each moment, what you would like to do, how you would like to be.

See if you can suspend old habits for the present moment unfolding ...

When it comes time to eat or drink something, perhaps see how slowly you can enjoy every sip, every bite. How do these flavors and sensations change from bite to bite, minute to minute?

When it comes time to bathe, consider going so slowly that you are able to lovingly acknowledge every inch of your body so slowly, as if you were a child noticing every inch of your body for the first time. It's so easy to begin judging this or that about your body ... but maybe this time you simply let those judgements just fly by like the clouds. Enjoy the sunshine that is alive in your body, the light.

When and if it feels right, consider going for a walk ... what is now being considered the best medicine for the whole body. Even more so, notice what a nice mindful walk does for your senses ... notice the shapes you see, the colors — even different shades of similar colors ... notice the smells and even tastes in the air ... if plants are blooming, perhaps gently nose your way in to notice their smells, even the smell of the earth beneath your feet ... listen in on the sounds around you, this symphony surrounding you and moving through you, this symphony to which you are contributing your own notes and sounds through breath, through steps, through your heart beating.

When the sun goes down, consider lighting a candle. Maybe even turn off all the lights in your house. As you strike the match, notice the light explode outward in the room. Notice how it focuses and dances some more on the candlewick. Watch as the wax below the candle-flame changes and changes and changes so slowly. Watch the flame, watch how it moves, when it moves. Watch as long as it feels right, before the flame goes out or you put out the flame yourself, and then watch and listen and feel into the quiet darkness some more.

When it comes time to make your way back to your bed for another night of sleep and dreams and rest, consider resting in bed, under the covers, as long as you can before sleep takes you more deeply into life . . . stew in the sensations of the day, of all that was awakened in you as each moment unfolded. What is this life?

Invitation 27: Consider a New Mandala . . .

If it feels right today, consider creating a new mandala. You can review the instructions for creating it in Invitation 3 and in meditating with it in Invitation 5.

What new insights emerge for you as you play with this creatively?

Invitation 28: Looking Through You . . .

Choices, choices, choices . . .

Consider taking some time today to be with the bigger moments of your life after ages 20 - 24, an age of assuming some stance into adulthood.

If you have not yet lived these years of life or even much beyond them, perhaps bring to mind your hopes and dreams for the future. What stirs within you, what bubbles up from the surface within you as you take some time to consider these future moments? Is there even a multitude of possibilities within you for your future? If yes, no need to decide right now which path you might choose. Instead, can you let them all unfold in your imagination . . . maybe in much the same way as the previous invitation to being mindful of a single day? Let them all be, perhaps consider journaling about them.

If you have lived some years beyond ages 20 - 24, consider taking some time to be with memories from these years. Maybe consider sitting awhile to see what bubbles up from the surface within you. As always, no need to judge any of these moments . . . though many of them might be charged with emotions of joy or of pain. Perhaps simply be mindful of your feelings and sensations in your body as you remember. If it's helpful, look through old photo albums, family movies, scrapbooks, letters, anything from past years that is stacked up in your house or nearby.

What gold is there here in your past, in the vast rich soil within you, that might be helpful to be with for awhile?

As you look into these moments that have all helped bring you to this present moment, is there a past moment of your adult life where you might find yourself wanting to sit down with this version of yourself and have a conversation? You might consider this conversation through journaling about it — maybe one hand writes for one age, the other hand writes for the other age. You might consider having this conversation meditatively — guiding yourself into a moment of relaxation and then remembering yourself at this age and being with this version of yourself. See if you can do more listening to that younger version of yourself . . . what does this version of yourself have to offer the present-version of yourself? You might be surprised how wise you were then, at that age!

There might even be a moment from your adult-past that is longing for some love from you now. How might you find a way to offer this past-version of yourself some love, some tender compassion? There are so many ways . . . again meditatively, maybe creatively through a poem or artwork or song you might compose that gives voices to these versions of yourself — past and present. See what comes forward for you . . .

Invitation 29: An Invitation to the Larger Present ... Past

Consider perusing a national/world newspaper ... something with a scope larger than your hometown or your nation. Take some time with it, and no matter your stance on this story or that, see if you can feel into the story, into the lives of the people of each story. There will be a temptation to want to be judgmental about this or that, whether in the slant of the story, in the people's actions and reactions. See if you can sink your hands into the rich soil of the story beneath all of that, the gut-level realities of each person you encounter. Notice photographs, linger with the ways people share their story through quotes, wonder. If you can, look deeply into the eyes of the photographs, or if their eyes are not clear, maybe close your own eyes and imagine theirs, imagine looking into theirs. Maybe with an older person, wonder what she or he might have been like as a child. What life might have been enjoyed and celebrated with this person? What dreams might this person have brought into reality? What dreams might have been stifled? What life is there here in this person — even with all the pains and wandering valleys of life?

Allow quite a bit of time with this, if you can. What is there here to discover in the stories of the people of our world?

Invitation 30: Teenage . . . ?

Consider taking some time today to be with the memorable moments of your life between ages 17 and 19, an age of discovering a larger world.

If you are in the midst of these years, perhaps take some time to be with what these years have been like for you . . . in the midst of the roller-coaster life, what have been some of the thrills? the twists? the turns? maybe even moments when you have been confused or hurt or fearful of what is coming around the bend?

Consider journaling about these years, and then find someone you trust — a devoted aunt or uncle, a neighbor your trust, a loved coach or teacher, anyone who is well-beyond these years, a generation removed from you — and interview that person about what it was like being a teenager in their life and maybe what advice they would have for teenagers today to move through this passage of time. Invite them to tell stories about their teenage years, about funny moments and scary moments and, if they really trust you, embarrassing moments that they now can laugh about.

If you have lived some years beyond these late teenage years, consider sitting with these years for a time. As you are gentle with yourself, what memories come from within you? Let them all come and see what happens within you as you remember. What were some of the joys and freedoms of this age that you'd like a taste of today? What are some of the confusions and troubles of these years that you'd be happy to leave behind? Are there things that used to embarrass or greatly bother you then that do not anymore? As you grew into young adulthood, what things or parts of yourself did you feel the need to hide or were difficult for you to share with others? How has life changed for you since then?

If it feels right, perhaps there is some version of yourself from these later teenage years that might appreciate some time with your adult-self now. As we did in Invitation 28, consider some ways to offer this adolescent-version of yourself some love, some mindful compassion.

Invitation 31: Being in Love with Our World

Consider sitting with another newspaper today — again, something that encompasses some significant world-news, in story and image.

As you rest awhile with these stories of today, as you sit with the people and all that is happening for them, the heartbreak and the joy, as you notice the ripple-effects of these people's stories with their families, their friends, their mother, their father, their neighbors, all who know them, what do you discover about this life?

As you rest awhile with them, with this community that is humanity, is it possible to share love, compassion for them and their loved ones? In our culture today, when someone is going through a tough time, we tend to say things like "I am thinking of you" or "I'm praying for you" or "my heart goes out to you." Is it possible, with these strangers you are encountering in these news-stories, to think of them, to pray for them, to feel love from within you reaching out to them, even though they might be half a world away?

See how long you can stay here with these people, these new friends in the larger, whole wide world . . .

Invitation 32: ages 11-12-13-14 . . . awakening

Consider being with yourself during the moments of your life as something began awakening in your body, some new way of being in the ages of 11 - 14, or whenever something about this larger life awakened within you through adolescence. Allow the moments to come to you, to arise from within you, your guts, every cell of your body. Again, maybe a particular version of yourself at this age would appreciate your present-self sitting down with her or him, being with, tenderly loving this version of yourself into life. What images or sounds or smells or tastes come to you as you remember? Stay here with this younger version of yourself, your life. What might be waiting for you, your adult-version of yourself, to embrace, to hold tenderly in your own arms?

Listen in on and do whatever feels right for you now.

Invitation 33: Who needs love in your life . . . now, in the past, in the future?

Consider bringing to mind the people of your life . . . whether these people are on this side of life or the next. Maybe they have yet to be born into this life, though you anticipate them.

It might be helpful to list them out, all of these people who have been important for you in some way . . . friends, family, neighbors, teammates, acquaintances with whom you might have spent only a moment or two though your lives have never been the same as a result of that encounter.

No matter what our history has been or will be with these people, can we offer them love — in much the same way we did with the people of the world in Invitation 31.

Rest here awhile . . .

Invitation 34: ages 5-6-7, beginning again

Moving more deeply into our treasure-chest of memories, see what you can recall from your earliest years of memory in this body, in this life. What do your senses have to offer these memories? Maybe there are particular tastes of things that swim back to you from favorite dishes, particular smells wafting through your home or neighborhood. As you close your eyes and take them in, maybe remember the layout of your home at these ages . . . where furniture was, where people gathered, laughed, cried. Where did you like to hang out? Did you have any playmates who were important for you, or maybe you longed for someone who understood your ways of playing? What sounds surround you in your home, what feelings? It might be easy to immediately judge them all as joy-filled or anxiety-filled . . . but as you rest here awhile, see if you might be able to get a feel for the simple pleasures of life and the pains and anxieties that you faced, maybe that we all face in some way through being human and discovering ourselves in a larger world that does not always make sense.

If it feels right, let your imagination wonder through your neighborhood, your school, everywhere and anywhere you feel called to explore.

That very young version of yourself might need you, an older guide, to hold her or his hand to explore these places, to remember these places. These younger years can be times of such great excitement in discovering life's joys, and these younger years can be times of great confusion and sadness. How might you tenderly hold this child, this younger version of yourself, in such a way that gives her or him permission to explore freely and at the same time have a safe container, your presence, with which to be safe and secure and loved in whatever way seems right for you.

Again, if it's helpful, consider journaling about this — and maybe about any conversation with this younger version of yourself. It might be helpful for your dominant hand to write as the older version of yourself and your non-dominant hand to write as the child . . . you might be surprised by what this child might offer you as you explore. Consider asking this child what it is she or he needs right now, in this young age, and see what that non-dominant hand might express on the page . . . perhaps what you might feel like you need right now in your present life?

Invitation 35: A Colorful Practice of Embodiment

Consider taking a walk to enjoy some fresh air, the ability to move and breathe in this amazing body that knows when to breathe, when to pump blood through your body or digest food or even move or walk. Perhaps see what you begin to notice as you do bring some awareness to your moving body, to your breath, your heart beating, your digestion.

Take in the colors as you walk, even the different shades and expressions of the same colors, perhaps even the shadows and ways light expresses itself over these colors.

When you return, consider enjoying this meditation. Maybe someone might even be willing to read it to you slowly.

As you take some time to relax and rest awhile, feeling your body in contact and supported by something . . . a chair, the ground, a bed or couch, whatever feels right for you . . . take some time to feel that support. What areas of your body are in contact with that supporting surface? What areas are able to relax as a result of that support? As you scan your body from the inside out, imaginatively or even lightly with your fingers touching surfaces of your body that are easy to reach, are there some areas that you feel you might be able to relax a little bit more? When you find an area, maybe simply take a cleansing inhale and enjoy releasing a bit of that tension on a slow, full exhale. Continue with this as long as you'd like. (pause)

When you are ready, I invite you to take your imagination into the core of the earth, that molten, mineral-rich lava that participates in holding our earth together. Maybe you've seen images of volcanoes spewing that red-orange-yellow-rich lava forth into rivers or streams of fiery-hot flow over the land. See if you can take in those colors, those deep and bright colors of lava that give birth to so much life on this planet. (pause)

Over the years, as the lava cools to a dark or brownish-reddish-orangish-yellowish color, notice the greenery that begins to emerge from it, the seeds that find such richness in this new soil that might seem so impenetrable but somehow, some way opens itself up to receive the seedling. Watch as this green-life grows out of the rock, the soil, all the viny twists and turns and beautiful shapes the greenery makes as it all reaches out with leaves that unfurl themselves upward to the sky and grow and grow and grow. (pause)

Notice the sky that is the backdrop of these leaves, that beautifully bright hue of blue that blazes itself across the sky. As you look at the vastness of this blue-horizon, notice the different shades of blue near the corners that you can see, the corners that might be framed by land or mountains or sea. Take in all of that amazing blue of the daytime sky. (pause)

And when you are ready, let that beautiful blue of the daytime sky begin to transform itself into the brilliantly deep indigo of the night-time sky. Take in that brilliant color, how when you look into it, how it almost seems layered, like a box or a window you peer into that has no end to it. (pause)

And then let the stars and moon and planets emerge in that brilliant indigo sky . . . those lights of the sky so bright in a clear sky in the middle of nowhere but here. Take in these lights, the colors that emerge against this indigo backdrop . . . the golden and silver and pink and shimmering all-colors that radiate through this dark sky. (pause)

As you take in these colors, from the roots of the earth all the way through the furthest heavens, take some time to enjoy all of it, all of these colors dancing in their own ways. Take your time here, and when you are ready, very slowly bring yourself back to full awareness in the here and now.

When you have fully and slowly brought yourself back to full awareness, consider taking some time to journal or draw or even take another walk to let it all dance within you in whatever ways would feel good for you.

Invitation 36: A Story . . . Poetic Sands

I have been given many great gifts, two that I'd like to share here. The first is to be able to work with and tell stories for so many years, whether those stories are from ancient traditions and scriptures or personal stories or others' helpful stories that we pass on to one another to help us find our way in the world. The second is to be able to live in a city where scripture scholar Walter Brueggemann has retired and has shared his time quite regularly through lectures. He often speaks of the words of the prophets as "poetic eruptions", words that pour out of our mouths without any filter, words that come from our depths, our deepest urgings and longings, our truest speech.

I am reminded of a significant moment of eruption in my own life.

My last two years of college were marked by great learning and great unhappiness. I was unsure of so many things. I had spent my four years studying the humanities — essentially stories — unsure about how I would put this work and this learning to use. I was unsure of what all of this reading and reflection was calling me to do with my life. I was unsure of myself socially, and my way of dealing with all of that was to drink heavily at parties. I had a reputation for being a bit of a wind-up toy at the parties . . . "Let's get him drunk and see what he says and does." As I look back on it today, some of it was indeed funny, much of it very, very sad. I was trying to figure out who I was, who I am, all the usual searching of late adolescence and early adulthood swirling and mixing with questions about identity, about the discomfort of living in my own skin. I was in great pain, though I am not sure I knew it while I was going through it.

Graduation came and went, and many parties were there to be had. By then, I had figured out that drinking was no longer really working for me. At the big celebration graduation night, I left the party at 9 PM and went home to bed. I had had enough of all of this. Maybe some of it was the jealousy of the exciting paths my friends were pursuing: medical school, law school, graduate programs, exciting job prospects in new towns. I had been working part-time for a local social service agency and decided to stay on full-time for the next year. I enjoyed my work there, though I knew in my guts that I would not be in it for the long-term.

My friends must have sensed my building depression. David and Jacob approached me the day after the party and asked if I wanted to go on a post-graduation adventure. "Where? I don't have much money." Something in me knew I had to go. "We'll drive my dad's car and throw a tent and sleeping bags in the back and keep it simple." It was sounding better, easier. "But where will we go?" After a few not-so-great ideas were passed around, finally they exclaimed in unison, "Michigan!" My eyes must have rolled. "Michigan is a state, not a specific destination." But in their giddiness, we made plans to leave in a few days.

With a map in hand, we would drive to places that looked interesting to us: the University of Michigan, and then over to Grand Rapids, and then on to Lake Huron. We zig-zagged our way across the state just seeing what it had to offer. The weather was amazing, seventy degrees and sunny as we passed roadstands selling their bounty. We ended up in Traverse City and saw on the map Sleeping Bear Dunes. "What are those?" David asked. "Let's go find out," our usual response.

The sun that day set the air ablaze, the hottest day in some time locals told us. We drove into the park, a massive sand dune faced us. The park ranger greeted us, "You can walk all the way to Lake Michigan, but it's a LONG walk in the sand, boys!"

"Yeah, but we're men, and we didn't come hear to play in the sand. Let's go!" And off we went. We packed nothing with us — no water, no food, no sunscreen, no protection from the sun besides our t-shirts and shorts and sandals. We were pretty stupid.

The sand was hot. Very hot. We plowed our way up the first slope, a straight shot uphill for what, forty yards? Most tourists stop here and admire the view. We pressed on, off to see where these dunes met the Lake. I was tired immediately.

It should be noted here that I was in horrible shape, and David and Jacob were college athletes. My drinking binges often ended with a trip to the twenty-four hour donut shop just down the street from our house. My body rebelled with every step in the sand, and the memory of what we had left behind in the car echoed through me: the homemade donuts sent with us by Jacob's mom. Why were we torturing ourselves out here when we could be so much more comfortable in the air-conditioned car with delicious snacks and destinations to explore? My friends didn't take my hints, though. It was only later that I appreciated their wisdom.

We had trudged pretty far, and had seen no one else for some time. A huge wall of sand greeted us. We looked left for a way around it. No go. We circled right. Not any better. To get to the Lake, we had to go over it. David attempted first. Now remember, this is sand we were climbing. He got nowhere fast. Jacob gave it a try and figured out that we had to swim up the sand — catch it with his hands and pull himself over it before it slid beneath him. Jacob made it up to a solid cliff as David gave it another try. Sand was being kicked in my face as I contemplated why we were doing this in the first place. There was no prize for success here — and there are donuts in the car! Jacob continued up as David found a solid shelf upon which to rest and encourage. "Come on, man, let's go!" they both said to me. Oh, alright. I tried and slid down immediately. I tried again, no good. I could hear them scurrying off, felt the dry sand from above spilling down into my face. I looked up. David and Jacob were nowhere to be seen. Anger began flaring throughout me. I hated all of this. I heard another "let's go," not sure if it was from them or me. I started up again and flailed my way toward the shelf. The anger within me was hot, red, glowing. The inner dialogue of my life became conscious. "God, this sucks. I hate what I'm doing here. Why is my life so bad right now? What did I do to deserve this? What did I do to deserve any of this? This is such bullshit." Memories of my life bubbled up from within me, no apparent rhyme or reason to them. Without really noticing it, I was making my way up the sand.

The memories continued, memories of pain I had caused in others, through daily life, through drinking, through carelessness, memories of being hurt, of all the confusion that late adolescence brings. Maybe I had been addressing God through it all . . . God was certainly now the brunt of my anger, my one-way conversation partner. "Why did that happen? How could you have let that happen? Why this? Why that? Do you care about anything?" My most recent painful struggles came forward. I could taste the sickness in my mouth, the pain of my whole life. With everything I had, a voice erupted from deep within me. "FUCK YOU, GOD! FUCK YOU!" With that I hoisted myself over the top edge of the slippery sand and lay down on my back on the top of the sand cliff.

In the time of one breath, I looked over to my left. Jacob and David were running around the plateau like little kids. I felt the anger still simmering in my guts. What had I just said? What happened here?

Before I knew it, an enormous calm came over me. I felt a peace I had never known. I don't usually hear voices or anything like that, but a voice came. "Brian, it's going to be alright. It's gonna be alright." It was a most beautiful voice, soothing, peaceful. I cooled and relaxed back into the sand even more, those words salving the pain I had re-experienced. I let my body be completely supported by the sand, I let go — maybe for the first time. "It's going to be alright."

I don't know how much clock-time I let myself be there like that. It felt like forever. Jacob walked up, "You alright, man?" Uh, yeah. I wondered how I looked, wondered if they could have heard my rant, seen my experience. "We need to get David back to the car to eat. His diabetes, remember?" I got up, and looked at David. He had his hypoglycemic eyes, unfocused, distant.

We figured we had to slide back down — a little easier if we moved over a few feet. We all made it down safely. I felt a surge of energy flowing through me. I began running, full blast back to the car. They didn't know what had gotten into me. I didn't either. I booked it as fast as I could, new freedom and openness within me like I had never known, the years of beer and donuts jiggling at my side.

They met me at the car. David got his food and was better. I got in the back by myself and lay on the backseat. The clouds were fluffy against the blue, blue sky. The miles piled up on that car, the sky rolled on, I re-imagined what my life could be.

Part of me struggles with what I said to God; part of me knows I could have never held back those words — at least not for much longer. I suppose the Creator of the Universe can handle someone so small as me hurling cuss-words out. But I do know this, without those words (poetry?) erupting out of my mouth, not much would have happened in my life. And isn't this the way it is with everything? What is hidden deep within us must be said, must be told, and whatever it is, the Universe can handle it.

As I look at all the tragedy we have endured in our world in the past year, the past decade, the past century — all the senseless violence, the greed and the hunger, the aimless wondering that comes with comfort and "ease" while others wonder how they will even survive — I wonder from whose mouths the poetry will erupt to call us to what really needs to be said, realized, imagined. When will we be transformed together by words, just as the prophets of old have done and even continue to do?

Invitation 37: Ancient Lament . . . our ancestors' way of praying

Psalm 44: A Symphony in Four Movements

author's translation

Our ancient ancestors had an interesting way of praying. We can find evidence of it in just about any tradition if we dig deeply enough. Here is a poem written during the Babylonian invasion of ancient Judah. Babylon eventually enslaved and exiled these Judeans, and this poem is their reflection on that experience, of losing the land and identity promised to their ancient ancestor Jacob. See if you can feel how the emotions change from part to part of this four-part symphony . . .

<u>Part I</u>

God, with our ears we heard
our ancestors regaled us
the achievements you brought about in their days . . . the ancient days!
<u>You</u> crushed nations, drove them out,
You planted them
You acted like a shepherd to the tribes and gave them free rein
Not even with their own weapons did they inherit the land by force,
Not even their armed-forces had to rescue them
Yes sir, it was your hands and your arms and the light of your face that they truly counted on!
It was you, God, my king! Commander, Jacob's rescuer!
With you we knocked down our oppressors time and time again,
In your name we trampled those standing over us!
Because I have no confidence in my weapon,
        my weapons do not rescue me!
Because you have rescued us from our oppressors and as for the ones we hated you put them to shame
In God we sing all day long and in your name we praise forever!

***selah** = break in poem for music . . . and to prepare us for a coming change of voice . . . !*

Part 2

Yet you have rejected and disgraced and hurt us
You do not march out to fight in our armies
You turn back from the oppressor and the ones who hate us plunder for themselves
You offer us as food like little sheep and goats
And among the foreigners you scatter us!
You sell your people — and not even for enough!
You do not even get fair market price for them!
You pile up abuse on us to make us live there like that
Sneers and jeers surround us
You pile us up as clever sayings for foreigners . . . they shake their heads about us . . . they're not even the tribes (who pride themselves on clever sayings)!
Every day I am ashamed, disgraced right in front of my own face —
    shame is the only thing that clothes me —
From the taunter's voice, the blasphemer —
    from the enemy's face, the one who inflicts revenge!

Part 3

All of this came to us . . . we did not forget you!
We did not deceive your covenant!
We were not disloyal in the deepest recesses of our hearts, nor did we step from your way.
Because you have crushed us in the place of jackals (which feast on corpses after atrocities like war, natural disaster) . . .

You cover us in darkness!

If we had forgotten the name of our God, we would be scattered according to what we had mouthed to the foreigner's god . . .

Why wouldn't the True God sound this out, notice this? Because this one knows the secrets of the heart . . .

Because of you we are murdered every day, we are considered as little goats and sheep to be slaughtered!

Part 4

Wake up! How can you sleep, my master?! Get up! Do not reject your ever-lasting glory!
How can you hide your face? You have forgotten our humiliation* and our oppression!
Bowed down to the dust, the living breath within us!
Stuck to the muddy-earth, our bellies!
Stand up! Help us!
Pay the ransom price for us* ... for the sake of your loyal-love*!

Notes on Part 4's legal/covenantal language:

The humiliated ones = (form of) *anawim* ... about which the Jewish Law and the Prophets and the later tradition all refer, the ones that are humiliated because the economy does not provide for their being clothed, fed, cared for, the ones about which the Law and the Prophets demand care

Paying ransom = *padah* = the practice much discussed in the Torah about redeeming animals, first-borns, slaves, etc.

Loyal-love = *chesed* = covenantal love ... love and care obligatory due to the ancient covenant

Can you imagine a group of people in the ancient world putting the one they hold to be the Creator of the Universe on trial like this for all of the suffering that they are experiencing at the hands of their oppressors?

What stirs within you as you consider a community that laments, that honestly calls it like they see it, like this?

Invitation 38: A Modern Lament

God, with our ears we heard
our grandparents and great-grandparents have regaled us
the achievements you brought about in their days . . . the good old days!

Your compassion born like the womb of mothers
Your steadfast love
Your ever-steady faithfulness

How you formed us and made us a people,
A people who gather in your name – Christians and Jews and Muslims and
Buddhists and Hindus and agnostics and so many people, all your people.

In your name, I AM, we boasted all the day long.
You are the Great I AM!
In you we put our trust.

Yet you have rejected and disgraced and hurt us,
You do not take care of us one bit!

You raise up prophets for us – and yet you stand by and watch as they are
slaughtered by the Powers who cannot hear the Truth:

Jesus
Gandhi
Martin Luther King, Jr.
Malcolm X
Bobby Kennedy
Harvey Milk

Oscar Romero and Rutillio Grande
The UCA Jesuits of El Salvador and their housekeeper and her daughter
Maura Clarke and Ita Ford and Jean Donovan and Dorothy Kazel
Dorothy Stang
Franz Jagerstatter and Dietrich Bonhoeffer
Jeremiah
Socrates
The giants of old . . .

Thousands and thousands of men and women and children who have stood their ground in your name throughout the world! And all of them dead!

You lead all our prophets into speaking the truth and see what happens to them . . . !
How are we to stand up when we see them dying before our eyes?
You make us retreat, run from the Powers that hold us back.

Wake up, I AM!
Unmask these Powers that we may be redeemed: make Hierarchy and Patriarchy and Greed bow down at your feet.

Do you not see how they rule over us?
It is you we want as our king.
It is you we want as our president.
It is you we want as our leader, as our lord of life.

Have you fallen asleep so long that you no longer see our brothers and sisters clinging desperately to survival . . .

Earthquakes and hurricanes and tsunamis and floods and droughts only give us TV images of the desperation that wracks the poor <u>before</u> you let the earth swallow them.

Bombs and rifles and barbed-wire borders reveal the terror in the eyes of children who have witnessed too much, too soon . . . another generation scarred, terrorized, frozen.

Even in countries not torn by war and violence, you do not keep our most vulnerable from the harm of authorities we thought we could trust . . . our children placed in the hands of men and women wracked by addictions, and their authorities and ours who cannot hear the truth, nor speak it. And our concerns are dismissed as gossip by our authorities, by the well-fed, by the royal-robed. They do not even let us grieve!

Ah I AM, we know we are not off the hook. We know we enact the very same things, the very same Powers on a small-scale in our own relationships, in our own lives. We fall victim to demons of depression and malaise and confusion, the same demons that wrack our leaders. We are lost. We do not know what to do.

Wake up, I AM! How dare you sleep during all of this?! Get up!
How can you hide your face?
Can't you see how we are down in the dirt! There is nothing we can do!
Stand up for us! Help us!
Do something, anything for us . . . for the sake of your love of us!

Invitation 39: Crafting your own lament, from your life, from the newspaper, from history

Consider crafting your own lament as the ancients did. Maybe you use the four-part process that they did, or maybe yours is more of a rant, an eruption.

It would be helpful to write it down so that you and others can gather in Invitation 40 and work with these modern, personal laments.

If this template from our ancestors and these questions are helpful, please use them to help you craft your own lament.

Part 1: What are some things you have heard from others about how they have been cared for during their struggles? Maybe there are some times in your life when you have been cared for . . . even in the midst of disaster, were there moments when you came through unscathed?

Part 2: What are some moments in your life now or in the past when you have felt abandoned, when you feel like you have had to shoulder too much difficulty, when you have had to carry something painful? What are some moments in the life of the larger world that have been just awful, terrible tragedies you have witnessed or heard about or studied in history or more recently in the news? What has been just too much to bear?

Part 3: What do you feel like you have done to try to alleviate such suffering — in yourself or in the lives of others — though maybe you feel like you tried so hard and others just stood by and did nothing? Describe how you have felt in such moments when you have tried to do something to ease the situation but to little or no avail. Do not mince words here. This is not a time to be nice and hold back — let it rip from you. If you are angry, give voice to it. If you are terribly sad, give voice to it. It might even be helpful to shout all of this out if it does not make its way to the page as easily as you'd hoped. If you worry what others might think, try shouting in your car with the windows rolled up. What words — even types of words — are most helpful here?

Part 4: What words would you use to rouse others to help, to know about how you feel, to do *something* about what you are experiencing or witnessing? What might you do to nonviolently wake people up to realize what is happening all around us? Do you have the courage to take some responsibility — even the slightest bit — for your part in any of this tragedy? Is it possible some tragedy that you/others have experienced so terribly is being re-enacted by you onto others?

Let your time crafting this lament be playful . . . it might roll out of you in minutes, or it might need a few days. **We recommend not moving on to the next invitations until you have something here that satisfies you about how you truly feel or have felt.**

Invitation 40: A Communal Liturgy of Lament . . . and a communal reflection on it

Take some time to gather with companions who have also worked with these invitations to lament, who are ready to give voice to such laments together.

Find a way to gather that feels right for all of you — maybe you enjoy a meal together before or after your time together. Maybe your gathering in a circle to share this time together invites a sense of holding space for one another.

It would be very wise to be grounded, embodied during this invitation . . . take some time to sit together in the silence, maybe use one of the more calming meditations offered from earlier invitations in this collection, maybe one of you would like to craft your own guided-meditation that allows your whole self to be present to one another. Take some time to prepare, to allow.

When it feels right, give each one of you space to proclaim your laments one at a time. It might be nice to receive each lament with some silence, with an opportunity for everyone to feel into each other's words without any conversation quite yet. Can you all sit with this public expression of pain for awhile? What happens within us, within the group as we give each other this space to speak, to be heard, to allow something new to be born from the recognition of the ashes of the past?

After each person has had the opportunity to proclaim her/his lament, perhaps take some minutes to rest there in the quiet. And when you all feel some sufficient time elapsing, have some conversation about this experience of working with lament. Why would the ancients do this, an actual practice of their prayer-life, both individually and communally? What happens within us as we speak what we know and have felt?

It's all very easy to lay all of our pain on someone else or some system or some group . . . and indeed we might have been terribly harmed by another. And we might not ever be ready to forgive someone for what they have done. The question of lament, maybe, is this . . . can we begin, after we cuss out the Creator of the Universe or whomever else we find responsible for our pain or the world's pain, can we honestly admit we have done some terrible things too, and in our truth-speaking and emotional rant, can we find some interesting solutions emerging for us to consider? Sometimes it's in our screaming into the air that the small voice within us can be finally heard, that well of wisdom that patiently waits for us to listen. Sometimes it's in our own eruption that the silence afterward can finally be heard.

What happens for you?

Invitation 41: From Where Do the Words Come?

We never really know, do we, when our training, our words, our wisdom — some new way of seeing something, saying something — will be called into play?

Arrupe's experience in Hiroshima mentioned earlier in the Inspiration might be enough to give us pause that all the experiences of our lives just might be heading in some direction — as wayward as we seem at times. All of his training in medicine seemed like a waste once he entered religious life, but when the bombs on Hiroshima burned so many people, he was one of the few who knew how to care for the wounded.

From where do the words come, the words that will inspire hope, unmask hope, even in the most desperate situations?

Consider Cincinnati-raised Nikki Giovanni, her story ...

She had been professor and well-respected crafter of poetry at Virginia Tech for many years.

And then she met one student who disrupted her sensibilities, someone she knew was not quite right, someone who was becoming a significant problem in her class.

Nikki and the young man had their disagreements. Students stopped coming to class out of fear of the young man and his bizarre behavior. Nikki Giovanni knew something was terribly wrong with him, and knew that he had to be removed from her class if the rest of the class was to prosper. Adults in the university-community tried to seek out help for this young man, but legally there was nothing they could do.

And less than two years later, in his terrible disturbance, this young man walked the campus armed with anger and sprayed bullets all over dorms and classrooms. Thirty-two people died that day, seventeen more were wounded by bullets, everyone else no doubt emotionally wounded by the shock of it all.

Within hours, the President of the university asked Giovanni, the community's resident poet, to speak at a prayer service to gather the community together.

What do you say? What do you call upon to invite the fearful and the confused and the grieving and all to know who they are, to journey together, to dream a new dream together, to live beyond such terrible tragedy?

When you get the opportunity, consider watching her speech at this link: https://www.youtube.com/watch?v=UpZ0F1rGBjc

There are many versions of it, simply search for "Nikki Giovanni WE are Virginia Tech" and you'll find it.

How is it that we arouse hope within us when the deck seems so terribly stacked against us? How is it we can invite one another into our pain and move through it to live again, to live even more intentionally, with even more hope for the future as a result of the pain we have experienced together?

Invitation 42: An Invitation to a Bigger World, a Bigger Life

Consider the strangeness of life, the bizarre twists and turns and tragedies that we move through day after day, year after year.

Is it possible that something that may have begun badly can end in goodness? Is such a thing possible?

In whatever way ways we are able to imagine our world, our life, do we have the courage, the heart, to honor the journey?

Invitation 43: An Invitation to Returning to the Womb

Whether we get along with our mothers or not, they did indeed give birth to us. Perhaps there is wisdom in returning to the womb, to that world inside of a world inside of a world, a dream . . .

If you can, allow yourself to be comfortable. Feel yourself living within your own skin, alive in this moment. Notice how you embody this container, how you are alive within this body . . . through a cleansing breath, a heart-beat, a light touch.

How were you born into this world?

See if you can remember . . .

. . . some sense of being held within some life much larger than yours . . .

. . . inside some watery sea, and yet safe from so much . . .

. . . how you could dance in there, move with and through those waves, how you could reach out and find life in all directions . . .

. . . how you were nourished, kept alive without any help from yourself, how you were dependent on something larger than your tiny self . . .

. . . how you responded to voice, vibration, warmth within that watery world . . .

What are the hopes and dreams of a child such as this, a child alive in this nourished world?

Invitation 44: Roots

When life swirls wildly one way and the next, into what do we root ourselves?

Where is it that we can go home?

From what do we reach out and grow in the world — no matter the rain, the wind, the terrors of the night?

As with Nikki Giovanni's story a few invitations earlier, from where do the words come?

How are we being invited to gesture hope in our world, in our own life today? How might your life be different if you paused once, twice . . . five times a day to remember you are alive, part of something much bigger than yourself . . . to pause as so many do around the world?

What person, what people might be longing to hear the words — a story, a poem, a shout — that will free them, that will invite them into this rooted life that you have tasted, yes?

What aspects of yourself — when you were a child at 5 or 6 or 7, when you were on the cusp of adolescence, when you were a teenager, when you were (or are) a young adult, whenever you felt you were stepping over some threshold into a new age — might give birth to Wisdom in the here and now, to life in all its fullness?

Invitation 45: An Invitation to Pregnancy

Just as we were once in the womb, now we might recognize that we too are pregnant, that something is alive within us …

an idea

a question leading to possibility,

a dream,

a vision,

a love that is so true in this season of our life, for another, maybe even finally for our own self,

maybe even a real living child is finding life within us.

What is it that is alive within you?

When you have a moment to daydream, what comes back to you always? … something so real to you that tears might even well up within you that lead you to such longing for this desire within you, this hope for a new way of being in this world … something so real that even your night-dreams offer you symbols to awaken within you some new possibility …

What is this life you feel within you, this life waiting for you to nurture it, to feed it with your attention, to give it permission to live, to grow?

Our dear Iñigo offers words such as these, such advice for birthing …

Pray and meditate as if everything depends on you;
act as if everything depends on something more than you (depends on God, the Universe, by whatever name we call this deeper sense of life).

How might that change anything for you?

Invitation 46: A Remembrance

If it feels right for you, place your hands on your belly, on your guts.

Our ancient grandmothers and grandfathers knew a wisdom here about life . . . this life of intuition, of gut-level reaction, of profound knowing.

As you rest here awhile in the quiet, consider placing your hands in one spot for a few moments and then in another, all over your belly. Be slow with it all, this feeling into the life within us.

What gurglings, what images, what sounds and voices and feelings come to the surface?

The voice of the critic within us might come forward every now and then — even this far into our explorations and invitations — and like anyone with whom we do not get along, consider offering that voice some love too. Sometimes the critic quiets when we love it, like a cranky child. Sometimes all any of us needs and wants is to be held . . . .

And listen in on the voice of our inner knowing, our Inner Teacher, that voice that we have heard once, twice, maybe so many times, that voice that leads us to life, that voice that knows something deeper about what this life is all about, its goodness even in the midst of tragedy.

Rest here awhile, listen in on what is born through us in the here and the now.

Invitation 47: An Invitation to Birth

As we lazily relax here awhile, let us be with that pregnancy within us.

As we rest our hands on our belly, we can feel again and again the life within us.

Just when we least expect it, we can feel the water breaking, a world crashing in on itself to bear new life.

We feel the opening within us, and not too long, the idea, the dream, the question, the vision, the person, the human one, perhaps, beginning to break forth.

We listen to our own breath, now labored with this spilling forward.

We had moved within so long, now, these many weeks, seeds scattered within us, and now one, two, more coming forth, bearing forth, some new way of being in this life, in this skin.

We allow our breath to welcome something easier, to catch us in this moment of opening from within to allow something to come through us. We experience the pains of labor, of life spilling forward from within us. We breathe. We know.

Soon, the head begins crowning, ah — this one too has a crown — our common sharing of power, the crown we all wear and must bear in this life, the realization that we are all indeed equal, all who wear a crown such as this. It's a crown not made of gold or silver or jewels — something much more important and valuable than these . . . a crown of flesh, of blood, of life, of our common humanity.

And soon then, the child turns and then the shoulders, the belly, the torso, the beautiful legs that will root this child into the earth, into being alive in this skin.

You see the connection of this child still buried deep within you, within the mother of this new being.

Look into the eyes, not yet opened, this mouth, not even crying yet, still being nourished from within, with this lifeline, this belly-button of the world. For now, so intimately connected to some place within us, some nourishing place deep within. And one day, this child will walk, will have a life of its own, but for now, so tender, so gentle here in these moments.

Give yourself permission to feel it all, to feel this new life in your arms. Feel that connection still alive between you and the child, still nourishing the child from some place deep within you, feel it slowly begin to let go, to be released, so that this child now is a being all its own. Surely still nourished by you, still dependent on you for life, for love.

The child begins its first breaths, a little cough, a smile of sorts. And then the cord can be cut, no longer needed.

As you hold this child, and you nourish this child, this idea, this dream or vision or question, what can you imagine is now possible, for you, for this child, for this life?

As you hold this child close to you for now, as you know it will one day — so soon — have a life of its own, can you feel the gentle tug within you between nourishing this child's life and lovingly letting it go, one day, to live on in its own unique way?

Invitation 48: A Reflection on Stories

Of all the stories you have lived, experienced, witnessed in your life, what stories stick with you? What stories come to you whenever you pause? What is your tap-root?

What story might be told that will free us and free others to dance our own unique dance in the world?

Invitation 49: An Invitation to Nourishing

As you continue to hold this child close to you, can you feel its gentle heart beating? Can you feel the ways it moves and lives in your arms? What wisdom for life might we come to know as we embrace this child in our arms?

Pause here awhile and know such love as this ....

As you experience its growth exponentially every day, what now might be asked of you to nourish it, to keep it living and thriving?

How might you care for your own self, that you may thrive as the nourisher of this child, this dream, this idea now come to reality?

How is your life different through such a birth, such a spilling forward of life and love like this?

Invitation 50: A Reflection

Who are the people who have held you so close during this life? Family, teachers, friends, even strangers in some synchronous meeting. What have we learned from them, through them, through their touch, their gentle words, the gleam in their eyes that knows something more than we often know? What have we learned of love?

Consider pausing here awhile, being with these people in our own memory, in ways our skin has remembered their gentle touch.

As we reflect on the mothers of the world, those who have allowed life to be born through them, once, twice, many times, what might we learn from them, in the ways they allowed such life to come forward?

What is there to know, what is it we might be ready to know, as we contemplate a love such as this?

Stay with this love as long as you can . . .

Invitation 51: A New Mandala

Consider creating a new mandala as you close these invitations for now, as you begin again. You might review the instructions for creating mandalas in Invitation 3 and in meditating with it in Invitation 5, or maybe you have your own way now that opens this for you.

What new insights emerge for you as you play with this creatively this third time among these invitations?

If you have travelled with a group of people, your companions on this journey into the Exercises, consider enjoying an evening together, a meal, a creating together these mandalas or even one very large mandala, a sharing in words and silences and embraces, as you all see fit.

For what are you grateful in all your time together? What will you take with you, some gift from each person?

Invitation 52: A New Setting

As Iñigo makes very clear in his writings, there is no one way to move through the Exercises.

If we know anything about life and all these seven billion lives who walk this planet now, we would be wise to consider that there are seven billion ways to move through the Exercises. Sure, there might be some overlap, some particular Exercises might be helpful or beneficial for just about everyone. And just as sure, some particular Exercise might be helpful for only one or two people who walk this earth right now.

Consider writing your own setting of the Exercises for your own community and gather some friends from that community together to welcome a new life, a new way of proceeding in this life together ... and send us a copy of what you all come up with so that our VITALITY community might be challenged by the questions and stories you gather together ... so that we might find renewal in our skin, in our lives, in every breath.

Perhaps you might shy away from such an invitation . . . perhaps as Iñigo surely did for so long knowing his past. As Iñigo reminds us, though, through his own lifestory, perhaps it's only the scoundrels like himself — like all of us? — who ever make a difference in this world, people who have known hardship and ease, carelessness toward others and tender care, masks and authenticity.

Come now. Join us.

Be you — no matter the cost.

Leave the "perfect" behind, the "ideal," and know in every cell of your body who you really are ... infinite ... stardust ... light for our world, no matter our pasts, our future.

What would this life — this big, immense life of this world — be without you, without your vision and ideas and dreams and longings, right here, right now?

Epilogue

We went all the way to Montserrat, Manresa, Barcelona, Rome to know more of Ignatius' experience . . . and it was beautiful. But for what? The journey to knowing is within . . . .

A Treasure-Trove of Stories . . .

from the friends of VITALITY who shared their stories at our Spiritual Exercises storytelling gatherings . . . friends from all ages and walks of life . . . may our stories inspire you to tell yours!

What is your story?

A Story — Dan Price

Last week, my wife and I stopped for lunch at a Panera near the local Mall. We placed our order, found a booth, and began eating and conversing. As we were finishing. I noticed a man entering by the side door. Hmmm. He was not dressed too well and then it struck me. Ah yes, he is one of those street persons who stand at exit ramps of the Interstates or at busy intersections with a cardboard sign: "Homeless, Need Food\Work."

He is going to ask for some spare change from a few patrons. A deep emotional chord is struck. Verbalized it goes like this: "Oh no, not here, not on our turf. This practice can really bring down the quality of life in this area." And my imagination raced along with further thoughts, "What kind of reputation will we acquire?" "Will we be lumped with the exit ramp crowd?" All that and more flashed through the mind in just a second or two.

Don't mistake me. In no way did I feel physically threatened by this person. I did, though, feel threatened in terms of, well, property values. I had flashes of memories of how various neighborhoods had declined—you know, stores boarded up or closed or sold to a cheap dollar store for those with less income. All that decline starts in small steps, you know, and this is one of them!

I carefully watched his steps. Yup, he sought out the far corner of the eating area to approach a woman sitting by herself. He exchanged a few words with her, then there was a shake of the head and he proceeded on, his eye scanning the next "candidate." Yup, another professional looking woman, sitting alone and closer to the door. Same kind of exchange!

At this point, I sprang into action. No, I did not confront the person to tell him he was not welcome here or, at the other end of the spectrum, where he could find assistance (if in fact, he really did want physical assistance). I spotted the manager behind the counter and leaned over to tell her what was transpiring. I pointed him out and told her in a quiet voice what he was doing. The manager? She blanched, quickly responding that she'd immediately take care of it.

As I continued watching from afar, the man had just approached his final encounter, an older gentleman working on his laptop. Ah, this time the man was successful. The older gentleman was just now closing his wallet. And then puff! The man, the beggar, was out the door. He certainly knew what he was doing: a side entry door, confidently approach just a few patrons sitting alone, then a quick and unobtrusive exit!

Later that afternoon, I recalled the incident with my wife who in turn pricked my conscience. That man was an individual, not a representative of a particular class. I had no knowledge, she told me, that he would be back in this area and besides what if he were. Most tellingly perhaps, she reminded me of a current saying, which is associated with Pope Francis. Francis is encouraging that we "create a culture of encounter" with the poor, not just a check nor a handshake, but a looking into the eyes of each other.

* * *

Such is my story. Upon reflection, I am reminded of our various movements of prayer found in the Exercises. Was this a discernment of my less than perfect self? Was it my looking at the face of Jesus and refusing to respond, even with pity or more basically just "letting him be"?

My conscience was pricked for telling the management about him and presuming they would remove him. No, Panera's management does not want him in this store—it's bad business because they have an atmosphere to create and an image to maintain. (Besides at the end of the day, Panera is noted for helping out food banks with day-old bread. On an institutional level, the company and this store do provide for the poor.)

You know, upon even further reflection, I am not afraid of "getting my hands dirty in working with and for the poor." I cringe at displays of unnecessary luxury and wasting of food. Indeed, I even volunteer at our local food pantry and have a reputation there for making people feel welcomed and comfortable. Ah, and there I am on their turf and I am their guest. I mind my manners. More importantly, I am free to come and go from that turf as I choose.

It was that awareness of economic class—neatly summed up in the pithy phrase "there goes the neighborhood" which I had experienced. I am ready, even happy, to work with the poor but on their turf, not on mine. Don't threaten my standard of living! Don't damage the reputation of my section of the city!

Now, what would I do if I encountered the same scenario again? What would I do? To be honest, I don't know.

Prayer:

Jesus, help me to discipleship.
Jesus, help me to integrity.
Jesus, help me to answer the invitation to join you in creating a "culture of encounter."

A Story — Tamilla Cordeiro

Growing up in communist Russia, my family may not have had food, but we did own a German Christmas candle carousel. And although religious practices were strictly forbidden (with a Muslim father and a Jewish mother, what would we have celebrated anyway?), the Russian people were allowed and encouraged to celebrate New Year's Eve. We had a New Year's tree, decorations, Grandfather Frost (the Russian Santa Claus), a special dinner, champagne, and presents. Or at least I was told there were presents, a tree, a dinner. Living in poverty, I actually don't remember any presents I received on New Year's Eve, either because there weren't any or because they weren't nice enough to be memorable. If only Amazon.com delivered to communist Russia...

What I do remember is the German carousel.

Every year, my mom would dig it out of storage (what does storage look like in a one bedroom Soviet-era apartment?), take it out of the box, and diligently start assembling the pieces. Up went the sides of the "pyramid-like" structure. Then the fan blades were inserted. The deer placed on the rotating part of the carousel. And finally the candles, one at each corner. As she lit the candles, my brother and I would sit quietly, mesmerized, waiting. After a few minutes, the smoke from the candles would rise, and the fan would begin to spin. Then the carousel would start slowly moving, around and around. The deer holding on for dear life.

Every year this was quite an event. As we became older, I would still ask her to pull it out of storage, even though we were no longer poor and could afford other forms of entertainment. The carousel became old, slightly broken, and hard to assemble. But my memories of it never faded, and when my own children became old enough to appreciate the carousel, I asked my mom if she could pass it on to my new family. I hoped that it would mesmerize my children and make an imprint on their childhoods, as it had on mine.

Whether or not it will capture their attention is still yet to be seen. My husband and I managed to burn the majority of the fan blades, and basically break the entire carousel. However, my children are still young, and there is plenty of time for this tradition to grow. After all, Amazon.com can deliver a new carousel straight to my house in as little as 2-3 business days.

A Story — Brian Geeding

Sometimes everything works out so perfectly, so unplanned, that we can't help but to look to the heavens in complete awe and gratitude. I had one of these moments recently while visiting my sister Stephanie and her family.

My sister and her husband have three young boys. Jay is 6 years old. Matthew is 4. Adam is 2. Jay celebrated his 6th birthday a few weeks before I arrived. One of Jay's big presents was to go to a Harlem Globetrotters game with my sister, which was on the Saturday I was there. Stephanie and Jay left for the game around one in the afternoon, which meant that my mom and I would be with the other two kiddos for the rest of the evening. Matthew, the 4 year old, was a little disappointed that he wouldn't be able to go to the game, so I told him that we would do something fun while they were gone. "Matthew, we will go on our own little date." I suggested a few things to him — the candy store, the park, the library. We decided to first go to the park. Before we left I told Matthew to bring anything that he wanted to play with and put it in the trunk. He took a whiffle ball/bat, his bike and a soccer ball. As I was closing the trunk Matthew said, "Wait, I want to bring this bucket too." I wasn't quite sure why he chose the bucket, but it sure came in handy later on.

As we arrived at the park, which was about a 15 minute drive away, there were cars parked everywhere. I had never seen the park this crowded. I saw a few bouncy houses in the distance and I figured there was a private party. "Shoot Matthew, I don't think we are going to be able to go to this park." My mind started to scramble as what to do next. Matthew responded, "Don't worry, Bri, everything will be okay." When he said those words, I realized that he was, at that moment, a direct line from God. Something about what he said struck my heart. As a result, I continued down the road into the crowded parking lot. As I turned right, a car was pulling out of a prime spot and I swooped in. Our car faced the baseball fields and I saw hundreds of kids lined up along the perimeter of the field. I then noticed a bunch of colored dots in the field — Easter eggs!

"Matthew, do you see what I see out on the field? I think there is about to be an Easter egg hunt!" I was in complete amazement of what was transpiring before us. "Matthew, we better get out there now because I think they are about to start." This is where the decision to bring the bucket came into play. God had planted the idea in Matthew's mind to bring that bucket. God had gotten us out the door at the exact right time to make it to the park one minute before the Easter egg hunt started. God spoke the words through Matthew that kept me from leaving the park.

We collected about 40 candy filled Easter eggs, got ice cream from a truck, received a free Frisbee, and walked around. Most importantly, we both were in shock of what had just occurred. Even Matthew, a 4 year old, understood that something profound and beautiful had just happened to us. "I can't believe all of that happened, Bri. This was the best date ever." As we drove home, tears welled up in my eyes in gratitude for the gift God had given us. Every day these God moments surround us and on this day in particular we had the eyes to see them.

A Story — Maureen Sullivan-Mahoney

A Legacy

My great maternal grandfather was born in 1864 to Irish immigrants. Somehow he made his way to Ohio. He was a printer by trade and had a strong belief in education and in being kind to animals. He had a cow, Bessie, that he dearly loved. He believed it was wrong to eat veal because of the cruelty associated with how the baby calf is raised and then slaughtered. At age 40, when my grandmother was just nine years old, he died of pneumonia (penicillin had not been discovered at that time). I yearned to see a picture of him and Bessie but there were no pictures, just memories. As a child I pictured him as a compassionate and wise man. A man that I wished I could of known.

I grew up with my maternal grandparents until I was eight and a half. I also grew up with an Irish Setter by the name of Michael Patrick Joseph Sullivan (really!). He accompanied me in hiding in tents I made from blankets and overturned chairs, naps on the porch and romps in the back yard. My grandmother, Michael and I would take glorious walks down the street which ended at the banks of of Lake Erie. On one side there was a woods about a football field from the shore, where great exploring took place. As we walked along the beach we would look for pop bottles to redeem for money. If we found five bottles that would mean we would have ten cents to save. My grandmother would hand me the money when we left the store and I felt like I was the richest person in the world.

When I was young little turtles were for sale. I believe they are now banned. But, I was so happy when I got one. My friend came to see the turtle and we mutually decided that the turtle needed to be baptized. The priest house was three doors up from my grandparent's house, so off we went. The new young priest was very accommodating and blessed the turtle. He was so nice and receptive to blessing beings that we frequently visited him that summer with frogs, turtles, and a baby bird that fell out of its nest.

My mother was also an animal lover and was an easy mark to talk into taking in a stray animal. When I was older and living with her, I remember a kid down the street telling me about his white rabbit. He said his dad was going to get rid of her, as in kill her, if he didn't find a home for her. So...we hatched this great plan that I would sneak the rabbit into my house and up into my room upstairs. The boy gave me a huge bag of hay, some rabbit food and the rabbit's bowls. My mother was at work but I had to get this all by my grandmother. The boy helped me bring the stuff in my house. It took four trips. Although it was late summer and very hot, I put on a big sweat-shirt and stuffed the bunny under it, looking like a pregnant 11 year old. Fortunately my grandmother had dozed off and I got the rabbit upstairs without a hitch. I fixed a nice place with the hay and the railings that had gone on my brother's toddler bed. My mother came home and everything was in order, except I was on high alert. Dinner went well. Later we were watching a show on TV and some thumping sounds came from upstairs. First soft and then louder. Then they stopped. I was sweating at this point. Then the thumping started again only this time it was on the steps coming downstairs. My mother looked at me and wanted to know what was going on. I froze and could not speak. She went to the door, opened it to find a huge white rabbit staring at her! There was some commotion about the rabbit, some yelling, some punishment, but in the end my mother fell in love with the white rabbit and the rabbit stayed.

When I was ninth grade my mother finally agreed to let me get a dog. A friend of mine's dog had puppies and they let me have the pick of the litter. He was a little mixed-breed black and white terrier that I named Sean. We moved just before I went into the tenth grade. The best part was we moved eleven blocks from where my grandmother lived. I would take Sean on long walks along the beach to my grandmother's house and then back home again. Mr. Sean loved going to my grandmother's house so much that he would lay waiting by the side door for a chance to take off on his own. Sure enough a couple of hours later my grandmother would be calling for some-one to come get him (he would not make the trip back home but would whine to go home).

As an adult I shared my love of animals with my children. Their dad had not grown up with any pets and did not understand the need for pets in the home. But, in his heart, he is an animal lover. So there were dogs, birds, a bunny rabbit, gerbils, fish, cats and so on. On one occasion the kids and I were out shopping and a woman was heading to the pet store with a box of black manx kittens. Yes, we went home with a kitten, food, litter, litter box and things that a kitten needs. There were no cell phones then and I didn't want to disturb their dad at work (well, that's what I told myself). So there was the hiding of the kitten until I could share the joyous news of our new family member (tongue in cheek). I, in my haste, had left the bag of food by the side door. That was the first thing he saw coming in the door. I won't repeat what was said. For a moment I felt like the young girl whose mother had just found the white rabbit. We named the kitten Nicholas and he was with us for many years.

My granddaughter is being raised with two dogs. And how she loves creatures! She, my daughter and her dad go on many creature adventures. When I travel to see them I am included in these wonderful adventures. She has a great love for books, going to school and animals. She wants a fish but I have been told there will be no fish! I asked what would happen if I accidentally brought a fish with me on my next visit. My daughter gave me her "look"! I won't be bringing a fish anytime soon!

My great grandfather has given five generations, so far, a great legacy: his love of reading, education and compassion to animals. To my knowledge, I have never eaten veal, and neither has anyone else in my family. I decided some years ago to live my life as a vegan. He planted that seed in me.

A Story — Bridget Rice

It never ceases to amaze me how much excitement and nervousness I get watching my children perform, whether it's a play in the school auditorium or out on the soccer field. In fact, during their soccer games my feet act like they have a mind of their own and won't stay still. So it is no surprise that my stomach was in a bunch of knots while waiting for my daughter to complete her temporary driving permit test. We had actually attempted the exam 3 weeks prior, but Kathleen didn't get passed the eye exam. So here I sit waiting, recalling what it was like for me when I applied. I know I am more nervous now! She has been in there longer than last time so this must be a good sign. Suddenly a young lady steps out of the testing room. She walks over to, what I am assuming to be her patiently, nervous waiting mother and says;"I only missed it by one question." Her mother graciously smiles up at her and gives her that look, which to me is filled with understanding, love, compassion, and wisdom. They quietly walk away. I am filled with hope and gratitude. Finally Kathleen emerges and gives me the thumbs up. I am filled with joy. I feel like dancing, I jump up and give her a big hug — notice I do not give her my car keys. :)

A Story — Mike Eck

April 16, 2015 - Joy

The last time we gathered, I shared how your stories of joy reminded me of the joy / awe of opening presents as a little boy...

... and the joy created by my parents when we traveled to Lake Mills, Wisconsin and spent an entire week with cousins, aunts, uncles and grandparents in small, simple cabins near Rock Lake.

Was it the gift itself that triggered joy? Was it the Lake, or the fishing or swimming and when we were old enough the first time on a golf course?

I think now —- the joy came from the anticipation and in looking at the present ... at the gift, not knowing what it was. The joy came from ripping the paper and the feeling of surprise. At four years of age — I hope ... I hope ... I hope it's the red boat to play with in the bathtub.

I think now —- the joy came from being with my cousins ... from watching my parents have fun and be silly with their brothers and sisters and parents ... and now remembering the memories. The joy came from the surprise, the relationship and the experience.

April 1, 2015 - journaled in Spiritual Exercises - reflecting on "The Way of the Prophet" which was included in a daily meditation from Richard Rohr the week near mid-February 2015.

I am an analytic. I think about it. And then I think about it some more. I think about it sideways and backwards and then upside down. A spiritual director once asked me "Mike ... what does your heart tell you to do?" I thought for a second and told myself inside my head "I need to think about that for awhile."

I procrastinate, then I do. This must be the battle of the mind and the heart. My heart finally won. I was thinking about doing something important for a long time. I was still thinking about it when these Spiritual Exercises began. What was I waiting for? My ankle to heal at 100%? Weather conditions to be safe? The Spiritual Exercises to finish and then inspire me?

Thomas Merton nudged me, when he asked "What is keeping you from living life to the fullest?"

The Holy Spirit assures me that I will meet God when I encounter the poor, the slaves of the planet, those in need. I may not like what I see, hear or smell. I expect raw and unfiltered humanity from those who are served and from those who serve. Will I be surprised and find joy and love?

I was afraid that I would not be strong enough to face this reality. I was afraid that I would peek in, blink once or twice and then dash back to my safe bubble in the suburbs. I was afraid of failure. My fear was to not finish what I started.

Jesus said "Follow me" and "Do not be afraid".

Yesterday (actually March 31, 2015), I looked in, took my first step and said, "Hi my name is Mike - do you need any help today?"

While reading / editing Spiritual Exercise Invitation # 35
Journaled in Spiritual Exercises June 22, 2015

This reminded me of a freezing cold, dark and starry November morning night. I felt the presence of God as a meteor shot across the sky. God answered my plea and gave me strength to face my thorn, my demon, my third addiction.

We had gathered for a Breathing Under Water weekend retreat on November 16, 2012 in Oldenburg, Indiana. This day would have been my mom's 79th birthday. The group was mostly spiritual directors and a few of us with addictions. The holy ground and space is the home of the Sisters of Saint Francis.

Before this, a spiritual director guided me first to Richard Rohr, then in March 2012 to Psalm 104 then to my dreams.

I dreamed of entering a brightly lit stairwell that led me down and around and down some more. This led to a long walkway to a door which opened easily. I had entered the command and control center of a prison. A voice asked "How did you get in here?" My response was simply "I don't know, but it was easy."

I woke up to know that I had crushed those who loved me. A neighbor and addiction counselor helped me understand why I was doing what I was doing. I asked for help and God did. Tears and a trembling voice revealed to the circle the ways I knew how I had disappointed my daughter and my wife and myself.

The retreat in Oldenburg was the end and the beginning, the Omega and the Alpha. Over time, I gained back my life and my hope. I no longer looked at a bottle of wine the same way.

Some say "That wine has a lovely finish and the bouquet is extraordinary". I thought "I better finish that bottle before someone else does." When people ask, I just say "I hit the lifetime maximum while I was still alive."

Where is the line between addiction and passion and motivation and desire? Is there a difference in what drives an Olympic athlete and what an addict craves? There is a gate.

Matthew 7:13-14 "Enter through the narrow gate; for the gate is wide and the road easy that leads to destruction, and there are many who take it. For the gate is narrow and the road is hard that leads to life, and there are few who find it."

A Story — Carol T. Yeazell

In trying to untangle how I arrived at VITALITY Cincinnati, I remember the book *Soul Medicine: Awakening Your Inner Blueprint for Abundant Health and Energy*. The book presenting non-conventional healing modalities grabbed my attention on the library's new offerings shelf. Little did I know how much of an impact the book would have on my future.

Upon finishing the book at the coffee shop, I left to pick up my grandkids. Only moving a foot out of the parking space I burst out crying. Having no time to waste, I stopped for a few moments to consider the source of this visceral response. My answer came quickly: If I were twenty years younger (thirty nine) I would get involved in some area of energy/holistic healing. Done. I moved on with my day and my life glad I had read the book.

Two weeks later an invitation to explore holistic health appeared in the church bulletin. Given my powerful response to reading *Soul Medicine*, I responded saying perhaps there would be something I could offer the group.

I took advantage of the self-care practices and classes VITALITY offers: Healing Touch, yoga, meditation and journaling. I am privileged to volunteer on the spiritual care staff at a nursing home and offer Healing Touch to interested residents, as well as to friends.

Six years later my journey continues...

A Story — Shelia Barnes

Raising the Vibration. Using Yoga as a Vehicle for Personal, Social & Global Change

I had no idea what would come of this Yoga Teacher Training program, beyond the knowledge of yoga poses. Boy, did I underestimate the process! The program allowed us to explore the supposed founders, trailblazers & game changers. It's an evolutionary process to say simply.

There were opportunities for Healing Touch, Journaling, Storytelling with Spiritual Principles, which sparked further exploration as Kemetic Philosophy as well as Egyptian Yoga is part of my cultural heritage. We also explored the 8 Limbs of Yoga which falls into alignment with most spiritual teachings I have encountered.

We are more alike than different, I continue to discover.

The 8 Limbs offer a guide to the elimination of intolerance. How so? The very 1st Limb is the Yamas with have 5 branches which represent: Non Harming, Non Lying, Non Stealing, Non Hoarding & Brahma, the Hindu God of Creation, whose creative activity depends on the presence and power of a higher god. Brahma is genderless.

We stand witnessing the recent victory & legalization of Same Sex Marriages in this country. Let us not continue to overlook the almost complete annihilation of the Native Americans, horrific and longstanding effects of the Transatlantic Slave Trade, Jim Crow, Black Wall Street bombings, The New Jim Crow-mass incarceration of people of color, Prisons for Profit. Police Brutality & Abuse of Power, Crimes against Women & Children, War Crimes, and Crimes against Nature. These matters did not create themselves. They were created from one of the lowest vibrations of human existence – FEAR which breeds Intolerance. To look the other way, because the skin you were born into or what you believe is the 'Group Think' Norm or Right, is the same Intolerance that continues to fuel the violence against those slated as different.

We all come from One Source.

To my fellow yogi's, we began this journey a chance meeting of energy, manifesting as reflections of that Source. Unknowingly at times raising the Vibration in the community, Breaking Bread together — we had the best food during our classes. Walnut Hills Health & Wellness Wednesdays, Gardening, Healing Touch. We experienced some very amazing things together. Not always in agreement, but with Gentleness, Respect and Gratitude.

Each one of us uniquely crafted from our own individual experiences, developing the courage to adjust our Drishti/Gaze for deeper clarity, we find that our travels though not the same, but none perfect or even symmetrical. Embracing the gifts of the Breath – Prana, exploring the bitterness of the murky waters, which hold the roots from which the Lotus blossoms & blooms. No judgments, no comparisons. Recognizing oneself as part of the greater One Soul Self.

There is but one source of Air that we all breathe, One Sun that warms us all & the Planet Mother Earth who provides us with sustenance and Water, the same ones rain upon us All.

It is the right & responsibility of every human being to be allowed to strive to become their best possible self without restrictions. Through Self Reflection, stay on your mat — seek your own Truth, Evolve.

Evolution is the only form of Perfection I've ever encountered.

This Yoga & its 8 Limbs is truly a vehicle for transformation of Self, Society & the World.

Power to the People, Freedom for All, Amandala Awethu!

A Story — Theresa Popelar

This was the year I discovered *Rent*, the musical, *The Alchemist*, and worked really hard in what turned out to be two of my most favorite college classes (human anatomy and Christian ethics in healthcare) and realized I was indeed going to survive a massively broken heart as well as the unbelievably obnoxious friends I seemed to be attracting.

Looking back, I had myself quite stuck in a decidedly self-absorbed, insecure, and dramatic way, as only a 19 year old with the luxuries of time and opportunity can. Lucky for me, my path crossed that of two older and wiser women, Emily and Tracy, who happened to need an extra in their group for summer breakout.

Under the guise of service, we headed to the hills of West Virginia and Nazareth Farm for some serious transformation. Amazing what a week in nature, trying new things, overcoming fears, laughing, listening, making music, working with your hands, and being quiet can do for the soul. Welcome Home.

I gained an appreciation for a slower, simpler pace, hospitality, and a deepening of the showing up and taking care of one another that my parents and grandparents first taught me. I also got the music of Dar Williams and older siblings I always needed and never had, two things for which I am forever grateful!

Mostly, I continued uncovering more of me, what I really care about, my dreams and desires, and had some small but profound glimpses of what I might do next: choose not to go to grad school right away; learn more about intentional community and Catholic social teaching and craniosacral therapy; take guitar lessons; maybe more humanities classes and less science; consider the value of healing minds and hearts, not just bodies...

The farm and that particular community were a sacred space for me and a huge gift, the birth of many stories, connections, and a broader awareness of the strong support I have received and am called upon to offer. And as I've continued to re-learn the lessons of compassion, community, being present, laughter, loss, listening, moving, integrity, creating, shiny joy, peace, love, pain, and the delight of real friends who easily remind you of your better self, I realize the growing up I've done. Such divine mystery the how and why and when we get connected to the people we do.

* * *

I'm remembering a few summers back, when my little nephew, the sweet baby James, was about two and a half, just newly talking, and I had been away on a good but long and rain-soaked trip in North Carolina, arriving home late one especially warm summer evening. For some reason I no longer recall, I was dropping something at my parents where he and my sister were spending the night because of broken air conditioning. No sooner had I opened the front door (which is pretty loud) did he come flying out of his make-shift crib, into the living room, and hurling his little warm body at me, gave an "Aunt Theresa, I was LOOKING FOR YOU" exclamation. And with his little paw hands wrapped around my neck in a tight squeeze and his head soft and snuggled on my chest I was overwhelmed with that visceral love so strong it feels a bit scary. After shaking off my initial thought - how am I ever going to love my own not-yet born children this much? - and the beauty of the moment sunk in I realized how simply that sums it up. Aren't we all just looking for someone to be whole-heartedly looking for us? To belong completely somewhere: in vocation, relationship, as a parent, or beloved, strung together in abundant connection? Sounds practically perfect to me!

A Story — Richard Bollman, S.J.

The Daffodils.

Steve Carson was alert but a little groggy in the CCU division of St. Joseph Hospital. I met him there on rounds, Pastoral Care division, Jesuit priest in a dapper wool jacket above the Roman collar, and a little sign with my name. In training, learning the way to meet and listen. Steve had been rushed in by an ambulance, barely remembering if he had been unconscious, or just groggy from pain medication. I introduced myself. You do this as if life is normal and we are making our way at a wedding buffet, but he allowed for more serious matters, a resigned wink at the truth, granting in a worried way how bad off was he. His wife in the corridor outside the cubicle took me aside. "It was a big one this time, his third. I don't know how he even gets to the hospital with these things. With this one." And quickly she added, "he's not Catholic, I am. He's not much of anything. It worries me." "I'll stop by, look in on him," I said. You feel a certain power, being well yourself, no heart disease, you know how to listen. And I wanted to console the wife. Aggie. Fretful, able to see far past what might happen, it seemed. Funny underneath, tired of following out the implications of heart disease time after time, tired of being the earner of the living, a dispatcher for the Tacoma police. Competent and bright and ten years older than me, younger than Steve, and I wanted to console her, something in me was touched so simply.

Through our visits, Steve began to call me Bing Crosby. It allowed a little distance and a little closeness. He was getting used to the truth of things, the road of recovery being almost worse than the prospects of dying. And Aggie was there faithful every afternoon, after her work shift. She would pick up information from the nursing staff, hoping I might overhear, and wondering what I would make of a non-Catholic dying on my watch. At least I think that's what she wondered, but we enjoyed instead the irony of things. I thought to myself, how would it happen, if he died, and would I fuss with some sacramental reach, or would she want prayers for the dying, but it was enough, as far as Aggie was concerned, that her husband had warmed up to me, would call me Bing, and that she had an ally, something more than her grown son could be, he a minor league ball player, in training. He was used to the calls, the heart attack scares and the real ones. Steve seemed to me to have worn out his family, worn down himself, easy enough, or not, with life. And with dying. What did I know? I felt ready for whatever would happen, I felt skillful. And die he did, with no one present, on a break weekend for me, for Bing, and a call came from the hospital, "get in touch with Mrs. Carson ." There was word that her husband had died. And a phone number.

I think in some way she enjoyed, finally, being able to plan a funeral, which I agreed to preside over in her parish church, not his, not theirs, and we moved fast on that, how, yes, this non-believer can have a Catholic funeral because she was a Catholic woman and she needed it, wanted to settle things that way. And she had a priest. The son and his wife, Earl and Rosie, were the other chief mourners, and Aggie's friends from the station, her sister and her husband, and old buddies of Steve, almost ashamed that they had survived the drinking and poker games and good times with greater strength. That's what I remember, a quiet knowing that life has changed now, not ended, maybe not for Steve even, but surely not for his son and his pregnant wife, I saw that right away. They had plans, seemed free of something. And not for Aggie, I thought, life not ended. She has a good job, an outgoing way. Not yet fifty. I stayed close to the ritual, having passed through the actual death scene, untouched and unbefuddled, subsuming it all in the role of priest.

Until it was a week after the funeral. Not much less, but a week I think. So amazing how things happen, this time a call from Mrs. Carson, and she's downstairs at the hospital entrance at lunch hour to see me. Well you do this. You learn to care by following expectations, how the calls come, and then suddenly there is more to take in. I got in to the front seat of Aggie's car, expecting a thank you speech and maybe a lunch, the local wild salmon. But she held the car quiet for a few moments while I settled in and turned toward her. Her face was more relaxed than I can remember it being during the crisis and the funeral. And she said in the tenderest and most honest tone, "I just didn't want to lose the first friend I have made in my new life."

That, not death, was the moment for my real befuddlement, and a choice, a willingness to just go ahead and understand. That's how the daffodils began to be part of things. It was daffodil season in the Puyallup valley, near where her sister had a house with a deck, and that was one of the invitations filling out the closing month of my training at St. Joseph. Lunches too, and I thought, why not, I enjoyed Aggie, her company, her directness and simplicity, I think that is what I would call it, even still. She was ministering to me, to Bing, finding me to be also Richard. We went to the daffodil fields after an early supper with her sister's family. All the buds were mostly open, by the hundreds, thousands, the sweet fragrance of soft earth, the flowers, tall grass, and that evening, still visible, Mt. Rainier rising up over everything. A picture of the peak, an enlarged snapshot, framed, was one of the gifts she sent when I finally got back to Cincinnati. With this dear lady I found not only a friendly way toward me, an uncomplicated friendly heart, but also a wonderful sense of place, and purpose, hospitality, which lifted me in and around the hospital, softer in my own heart toward everybody.

A year later almost to the day I revisited the coast, my Jesuit friends in San Francisco, and my supervisor at St. Jospeh's a bus ride north, and Aggie. Earl and Rosie had misgivings about our meeting, but easily the two of us were not often going to have the chance to enjoy any time or stories. And our intermittent letters, expansive and helpful (before email) had given us a continuity to explore. We drove this time to Mt. Rainier itself, where Aggie had been a camp counselor. This weekend the peak was shrouded, but the roads were inviting, snow on all sides, and as we left the park we found a dining lodge for tourists. We had taken polaroids of one another, two apiece, and kept the one we liked better. We showed them to the waiter, and put them on the table. We seemed to be celebrating the larger life of the generous West, with a dinner of fresh trout, blackberry pie, and champagne, which was the only wine they had! I still have the picture. I found it just a month back. You never know when grace will come. She is sitting on the rail of a wooden bridge against the backdrop of a mountain waterfall.

After this, each spring the daffodils would come to my small community kitchen back in Cincinnati. My Jesuit friends and ministry staff would begin to expect it, around my birthday, in March, a good time evidently for mailings from the Valley. A precisely taped cardboard box. Two dozen tight flowers with directions: warm water overnight in a dark cool place. We used the walk-in. I used the ceramic vase a friend gave me. The next day the flowers started to open and stayed so alive and yellow and fragrant for over a week. We'd exchange a letter again then, my thank you, her account of life at the dispatcher's desk. Or word of her grandchild, and then another grandchild, from Rosie and Earl. A sweet hello from her sister, younger and prettier than Aggie, but more conventional, you didn't remember things the way with Aggie. Once when she invited me to a dinner at her own house, I think it was when I left the pastoral care office, she asked would it be suitable for me to just come in and enjoy her food, "the work of human hands," she said, being serious and hopeful and funny. It seemed effortless, how she helped my life. I did not save her letters, only this story and the photograph and the daffodil memories awakening in the cool dark place each spring. Six or seven springs maybe? More. I didn't save letters enough to know.

And for a year or two, with the blooms, the letters began to confess to cancer. Oh, I thought, no, this is awkward, this may be nothing, this is as yet unknown, this is Aggie. No, dear God. I didn't know how to say much. Because finally she began to write with honesty. March came and went several times. Never without daffodils. And I bless her willingness to let me know of her therapies, the nausea and mess of it, and her gradual surrender to asking prayer. No, I did not save these letters. Mercifully. Maybe for awhile. How much I was unequal to, even as I commandeered my role of consoler, something really she taught me to do. Asked me to do. I hope in some way finally there was a moment of easing for her, from Richard in Cincinnati. The letters, they became briefer. There were omissions. I wondered if Earl might someday write alongside her own words a straighter story? A more positive prognosis? A word of thanks even, that Aggie had a friend in her new life. But was it that, a sustaining friendship? You don't know. I felt I was keeping death at bay, writing back with a listener's ear and careful wordings. Being sorry. Being encouraging. Telling local news. Even asking about Earl, does he still play in the minors? Asking about her sister, and Mt. Rainier, is it visible this month?

And I remember how just "feeling sorry," and writing words, gave way simply to sorrow itself, silence, when one year the daffodils didn't come. One March. That March. And when did the silence begin for her? Sorrow came along with a resigned anger: I knew no one would write to me about the ending days, the funeral, the burial next to Steve, the mourners at the dispatching office. I would never know so much as a date. I visualized what I could. I zeroed in on the dull uncaring ball player, but what do I know? There could be enough in a mother's death to awaken something even in him. I met him only once. But it would have been nice to have more than an absence, a missed mailing. I see my arrogance, I find a little boy still waking up even now to Aggie being gone. And then I'm thinking she did not pass along my address. She knew there were no others to tell the story. It was hers, and she had given it. I'm thinking she knows so much now about what has changed, not ended. I count on it.

I want her to have everything, all of it changed and not ended, simply that. I come to see, even in remembering again, that her gradual surrender of illness and friendship and the flower mailings, it left room for her to have all that matters. Even so, I try to pull her back, the tourist dinner, the mountain waterfall. The drive away from her husband's funeral. I think of her, her funny voice, her tender ways, I think of this very often. More gratefully now, decades after. Thank you, Aggie, that bears saying. It helps.

A Story — Bailey Dixon

I came to VITALITY and Cincinnati in general on the tail end of a rough patch in my life. In many ways I felt like a shell or a little girl, but surely not a whole person. I remember the first day I was petrified. My experience in yoga was limited, and I thought I was walking into a lion's den of intensely spiritual yogi health nuts who could twist and turn their bodies in ways I couldn't even imagine. I was excited for the challenge, but the butterflies were going crazy in my stomach.

It turned out that my fears were ridiculous and the program was very far from the experience that my imagination had developed. The first day I realized that most of the people around me were just as green to yoga as I was. Sure there were some food preferences, but it wasn't a room of ripped yoga bodies; it was people of all shapes and sizes, colors, and creeds, who all wanted to learn more about yoga for their own personal wellbeing and had a desire to share that knowledge with others.

I can't say that sticking to the program was easy. I was in overdrive in all aspects of my life trying to make up for lost time and propel forward into the woman I wanted to be, and this program took a lot of time and energy, which I wasn't always prepared to take on. However, the journey was amazing. I had no idea how much I would learn in the past seven months on a spiritual, mental, and physical level. As someone who has explored many different types of therapy, I think our weekly meetings were often just that: therapy. From breathing techniques, to self-reflection, to creative writing, to artistic expression...it was a lot like rehab for the soul. Slowly my shell began to fill. I felt better about myself, like I stood for something. I felt like I had like-minded friends in a strange new place, and I felt like I had a purpose. As we learned the poses and different types of movement and yoga, I gained a deeper understanding of my own body and the human body in general, and what it truly meant to care for your bones, organs, and overall physical wellbeing.

I made many friends, some of my first friends in the area, right in our VITALITY classroom. We shared intimate details of our lives and spent many hours together, learning about each other's families and lives outside of the room. From the start, I admired qualities in each person, and though we didn't always see eye to eye, we were our own crazy family with all its quirks and unique personalities. I feel like in meeting these people and embarking on this journey together, I picked up a little something from each one. Whether it be grace or inner fire, I can honestly say I learned something from each and every person in our VITALITY class and I am forever grateful for it. Through this program, I was connected to a whole network of yogis in the Cincinnati area, from different teachers, other students in teacher-training programs, my fellow classmates, and the many people that we had an opportunity to do Healing Touch with or teach yoga to.

On Thursday I have the opportunity to lead a yoga class to a bunch of trainers at a local fitness studio, to show them what I have learned. If this try-out, so to speak, goes well, I will be hired on as a yoga teacher in a budding program at this studio. With everything I have learned at VITALITY, I feel confident, which is not a quality I had at the beginning of this experience. This program helped me to find my voice and awakened in me qualities that had long been hiding. I am grateful and proud to have completed this program and I look forward to the journey ahead.

A Story — Melanie Moon

In March 2013 I started on a journey to reinvent myself. I had come to the conclusion that if I lost my job, no one was going to hire a 60 some-odd year-old librarian. Most people do not fully understand and/or appreciate what we do anyway.

I obtained Leslie Sansone WalkLeader certification first then quickly moved on to SilverSneakers certification. Before I could get the SS certification however, I had to have National group fitness certification. All of these certifications meant nothing without American Red Cross CPR/AED certification and group fitness instructor insurance. After obtaining SilverSneakers classic and chair yoga certification, I quickly came to the conclusion that SilverSneaker's "chair yoga" was not "real yoga"! There was no way for me to afford yoga teacher-training so I put it on the shelf. No sooner done than I received an e-mail about the VITALITY program that was going to be offered on Saturdays rather than on Sundays as in the past. This, and the $50.00 fee, was a green light for me so I jumped right in.

Never in my wildest dreams would I have imagined what I would gain from this program. Not only was I introduced to a new way of life! I was also introduced to Healing Touch AND gardening! I started changing my eating habits soon after receiving my WalkLeader certification. It seemed silly to me to work my body and not nourish it sufficiently. Well, once you start eating properly, the next step to insure that you are getting pure foods into your body is to grow it yourself! I started a compost in my backyard but to this day, the canopy from the trees does not allow sunlight. Once I get that problem resolved, I am sure to have enough good compost to add to a bed or two. In the meantime, I love working with Gary, Sue and Betty at the St. James, Julie Hanser and Concord gardens.

My prayer is that not only will the exercise, yoga philosophy, Healing Touch and gardening benefit me, but also those with whom I come in contact daily. I have a mailing list of over 90 individuals with whom I share information about health and wellness once or twice a month. I offer chair exercise, aerobics and/or yoga at 4 different venues weekly and the Ronald McDonald House once a month. I am available and eager to offer exercise at women's retreats, early morning exercise in apartment complex clubhouses and exercise break-out sessions at business seminars, workshops and trainings.

I have just one more goal to accomplish. With the yoga certification under my belt, I am ready to focus my attention on my biblical counselor's exam and practicum. With that I will be ready to offer counseling in addition to all of the above.

Never would I have imagined that I would learn that pranayama ujjayi breathing would clear my mind and enable me to move and hold my body in ways never attempted before. That Samadhi (the eighth limb of Ashtanga yoga) would be a goal in life or even the ability to move from using all of my senses to focus (Concentration/Dharana) to gentle stillness (Meditation/Dhyana) would be a desire. I have had the pleasure of meeting Patanjali who provided a roadmap to yoga through Ashtanga, Tirumalai Krishnamacharya, the father of modern yoga who practiced vinyasa by combining body and breath and K. Pattabhi Jois who combined vinyasa and ashtanga. I have witnessed the body's energy by watching an object hanging from a string spin, stand still, or rock back and forth.

At the age of 62, I am proud to stand before you and declare the goodness of God who has enabled me to do all that I have done thus far in life. I am totally dependent on him to take me to my next phase as per Jeremiah 29:11 ... "I know the plans I have for you declares the Lord. Plans to prosper you and not to harm you, plans to give you hope and a future."

A Story — Jalisa Holifield

What yoga has brought to me over the last few months is a reaffirmation of the importance of self-care, a wonderful network of people and a chance to reconnect with family.

I learned about VITALITY through an e-mail from the Walnut Hills Redevelopment Foundation. I joined the class with the intention to force myself into self-care as I was working seven days a week between two jobs. I realized that I needed a way to make a commitment to my self-care. I had no intent of being an instructor of a yoga class and only had been a participant in the past. Paying for a class and agreeing to dedicated time towards community service was a great way for me to do this. I wanted to be more involved in the community and I saw this internship as a great way to get involved as well.

I found relaxation from Healing Touch and yoga and people who are dedicated to the healing process. I appreciated the accessibility of this yoga class and that it was community focused. I feel this model is true to how yoga is intended to be practiced. I was reminded that I need to be gentle with myself and give myself the same respect I give to others.

The other members of the class have left a lasting impression on me. As the youngest member of the class I was excited to meet people who had many stories and experiences to share. I find myself most comfortable when I am in situations where I can focus on learning from the lived experience of others, no matter their age. I am grateful to each of my classmates for their dedication to the group and their genuine care for me. I was fortunate to have the opportunity to see examples of what my life can hold by spending time with people who have accomplished so much.

Yoga also brought me the chance to reconnect with my family. My parents divorced in 2008 and I had not spent much time with them since. It was very hard for me to witness the separation of my immediate family and I was unable to communicate my feelings to them for years. My therapist challenged me to take tangible strides to communicate with my parents. In brainstorming about what to do she suggested inviting them to the yoga class as a way to spend time with them doing an activity that I like to do. The healing atmosphere helped ease my anxiety about how our conversations would go. To my surprise my family was excited about the opportunity and attended several classes, even bringing other family members along.

In reflecting on the yoga internship I can say that this time has enriched my life quite a bit. I am thankful for the people I have met along the way, the increase in awareness and practice of my self-care and to reconnect with family. I am enamored by the possibilities that lie ahead. I am thankful for what I learned and what I will continue to learn as I complete the requirements of the 200-hour certification.

A Story — Elizabeth J. Winters Waite

What I Learned During Yoga Teacher-Training

In order to explain what I learned over the past six months of Yoga Teacher-Training, I should first tell you who I am...or at least, who I was. My name is Elizabeth J. Winters Waite and I am an accountant. I am an accountant who gardens. I am also an accountant who writes, and an accountant who photographs flowers. Sometimes, I'm an accountant who sings, and can talk like Donald Duck and make hideous noises with a blade of grass stretched between my thumbs. I am also an accountant who mothers.

Or at least I was.

Six months ago, when we became Thriving Walnut Hills, and Brian pitched the idea of teaching Walnut Hills residents to become yoga teachers, it didn't even occur to me to take the training myself. I am a middle aged woman, struggling through menopause, and I'm an accountant! Accountants might falteringly take a yoga class, once, maybe twice, but they don't go through yoga teacher-training, they don't lead classes. Oh, no.

Before yoga teacher-training, I had taken a grand total of five yoga classes, each of which kicked my accountant ass and I never went back. Over the past few weeks, with this graduation paper looming, I have thought about what made me decide to join the ranks of the yogis, to become a Sweaty Betty.

To be honest, I thought maybe I could lose a few pounds if I took the class. I thought maybe I could ease the little ache in my back I sometimes have in the morning. When it became apparent that the class would be taught in the Walnut Hills Redevelopment Foundation offices, I thought I should take the class just to safeguard the company's assets. After all, that is an accountant's primary responsibility.

So there I was, on a mat, in our office, doing downward facing dog, every Saturday, for six months. Soon after class started, I found myself doing downward facing dog in my bedroom, every morning, curtains pulled, door locked, just in case. It became my guilty pleasure. And that little ache in my back went away.

I missed a few classes when I went to Europe for three weeks, by myself, but I made up for it by doing yoga in four different European countries, and taught my first five classes when a friend joined me for the last week in London. My time in Munich was terrifying. I was alone, in a country where I couldn't even read the street signs, and got lost every single day. Because I was learning yoga, I never forgot how to breathe. I breathed my way through my fear.

I breathed my way through learning how to use public transportation and asking for directions in a foreign language. I breathed my way through lost tickets and taxi rides through strange streets. I breathed my way through gut wrenching loneliness for an extrovert such as myself, with no phone connection to anyone I knew.

I breathed my way through and figured out how to revel in the change, the mystery, the excitement of becoming reacquainted with my own company.

After my trip, I moved. I moved from a house in the suburbs that I had lived in for 29 years into an apartment above a bar in a neighborhood in transition. I breathed my way through that, too.

I don't consider myself an accountant anymore. I'm a breather. My yoga teacher-training has taught me that I can breathe my way through anything; any heartbreak, any disappointment, any surprise, any fear. I can make it all better through the breath.

And now, I can teach you how to do that, too.

Namaste.

A Conversation:
A Context for This New Setting of the Exercises

In the spring and summer of 2015, when VITALITY offered the opportunity to participate in the effort of a new setting and new envisioning of the Spiritual Exercises, three people familiar with an earlier envisioning of the Exercises shared in the series of evenings: Richard Bollman, S.J., Dan Price, and Jean Marie Stross. The three of them participated in the early internships and directed eight- and thirty-day retreats at Jesuit Renewal Center (now: Jesuit Spiritual Center at Milford). They gathered June 28, 2015 for a special conversation and remembering. It is our hope that this brief record of their conversation might help to set a context from which this new setting of the Exercises grew, for many of us have surely benefitted from their courage in bringing forward the Exercises in new and imaginative ways. Indeed, how did it come to be that people from all over the world journeyed to Milford to experience the Spiritual Exercises there? So many of us have been recipients of their work at Milford and witnesses to the profound impact the retreat-directors at Milford in the 1970's, 1980's and early 1990's have shaped the personal growth of so many people in Cincinnati and beyond.

Dan Price participated in the first internship to form directors of the Spiritual Exercises in the summer of 1975. He had experienced the Exercises multiple times before that through eight- and thirty-day opportunities. Interestingly enough, he was working as an historian during this time in his life of the internship.

Jean Marie Stross participated in the internship in the late 1970s and continued to engage in eight-day and thirty-day retreats. Her interests in the Spiritual Exercises grew after making a thirty-day retreat the year before her internship.

Richard Bollman, S.J., began working as director of the retreat staff at Milford in 1981 after teaching English at University of San Francisco. He brought a fresh, holistic approach to retreat-work, and more will be said about that in a moment.

* * *

Jean Marie, Dan, and Richard shared in telling the story of how Vatican II (1962 - 1965) was the impetus for the renewal of the Spiritual Exercises. Just as Vatican II encouraged religious societies in the Catholic Church to re-steep themselves in the charism of their founders, Jesuits began wondering about the roots of the Spiritual Exercises.

What they found surprised them as they dug through the archives of letters by Ignatius and one of his right-hand men, Peter Faber. Ignatius, of course, was the first director of the Exercises, and as we know from the Annotations in the Exercises, his impetus was to work with the individual. That is to say, he met the individual where the individual was in her or his life, worked with their life experience and desires.

It wasn't until he became Superior General of the Jesuits after their founding that there became a "template" of sorts to the Exercises, and that was because Ignatius was no longer directing the retreats for people due to lack of time on his part. Other Jesuits picked up this ministry. Dan adds, reflecting upon his conversations with Jesuit historian John O'Malley, S.J., "Historically the primary reason why the early Jesuits began to give the Exercises in a group setting with preached meditations 4 - 5 times a day was simply that of man-power, too many people wanted to make them and it was no longer feasible to do so in a one-on-one basis. This was especially true for the numbers of young men entering the Jesuits. In 1540, there were 7 and by 1556, more than 1,000! However, the first retreat house for men was established at Alcala in Spain in 1553, that is during Ignatius' lifetime so he knew that this adaptation was on-going—and the 18th 'annotation' encourages that portions of the work can be used in a variety of ways. Overall, one can note that the Exercises were seen from early on as a valuable tool, which could be offered in a number of ways to strengthen and promote the relationship of the faithful with God." (For more insight into this, Dan recommends O'Malley's book *The First Jesuits*.)

This template of a more "preached retreat" became the expectation for the Exercises, for the most part, until Vatican II. One practice at some retreat houses was to slip a piece of paper under the retreatant's door each morning with the scripture of the day from this old template of the Exercises — with absolutely no thought as to wondering if this is what the retreatant wanted and needed at this point in her/his life or her/his retreat. Day 1's prompts followed Day 2's prompts and on and on until the retreat was complete.

As retreat directors began re-examining the roots of the Exercises in the years immediately after Vatican II, they became intrigued more and more with Ignatius' personalist approach of meeting people where they are and working with how their life-experience might be inviting them to reflect and grow.

At Milford in the 1970's, Jesuits Bill Creed, Gerry Grosh, and Gerry Hair pioneered some of this personalist approach to the Exercises, as did many retreat directors throughout the world. Grosh's book *Quest for Sanctity: Seven Passages to Growth in Faith* (Wilmington, DE: Michael Glazier, Inc., 1988) was influential for many. Other Jesuits and lay intern staff continued to "mine" the riches of the Exercises offered through the internships. Jean Marie reminded us that when Richard Bollman, S.J., came to Milford in 1981, "We put on the holistic glasses Richard offered us to consider. Richard said, 'A holistic approach doesn't mean you just do yoga and eat bean sprouts. A holistic sense has to do with realizing we are already made whole, and we are waking up to the wholeness we already are, and the Exercises help us to wake up.'"

As one way of awakening that holistic sense of the person, Milford pioneered offering massage therapy as part of the Spiritual Exercises experience. Today, massage therapy and a whole host of holistic-minded modalities can be found at retreat centers around the world. Art, poetry, imagery, guided meditation, music, dream-work, dance/movement and more became ways of engaging lifestory in the Spiritual Exercises. As Jean Marie reflects, "one grace of the Exercises is the discovery that there is an ongoingness to relationship . . . that God is always offering the 'more' of God."

The retreat team of directors and interns pioneered the development of a holistic retreat model with colleagues Carmen and Jim Neafsey, Tria Thompson, body workers Kristen Corcoran, Maurice Reardon, Ted Tracy, and other helpful people. They all expanded the available methods of prayer, focus, and relaxation in retreats offered at Milford.

The retreat team had the opportunity to work with so many people doing interesting inner work through workshops held at Milford, and the program at Milford was richer for it. Howard Gray, S.J., and Fred Maples, S.J., were much-loved presenters who greatly influenced the Milford retreat team. Gray developed the relationship between the Exercises and social justice, which also became a further emphasis for the Milford team. Maples was a Jungian who worked with dreams.

Before each retreat was offered, the directors and interns would gather and begin the retreat together before the retreatants would even show up. They asked one another, "How are you as you're coming to this event? Who is the person (you) who has arrived here for this retreat?" It was their way to be real with one another, to be faithful to the inner work that is required to mindfully lead someone else doing their own inner work through the Exercises.

Dan offers that his work with the Exercises has helped him "have a sense of being grounded, an ability to listen and hear what might be going on underneath the surface . . . this has greatly affected my teaching. And through it all, listening to others' stories has helped me all the more to understand my own story."

Richard offers that his work with the Exercises has helped him and others "not to be afraid or embarrassed of areas of unfreedom in our own story — not to fear it — to know that it all does not need to be finished up in this lifetime."

Those of us living in Cincinnati and those who traveled far and wide to participate in the Exercises at Milford in the 1970's and 1980's and early 1990's have been given a great gift through this personalist approach to the Exercises pioneered by so many people mentioned in this interview and many, many more who took the internship at Milford or worked as staff members for the retreats. Those of us engaging the Exercises today stand on the shoulders of giants. We at VITALITY can only hope that this new setting further invites people into a taste for more, the *magis*, the discerning heart that Ignatius so thoughtfully invites us to discover in our daily lives.

Around the World, Around the Seasons
Four Recipes, Four Settings

each recipe serves 12-15 people
main dishes use a large slow-cooker for ease
all recipes are plant-based, gluten-free
we try to buy organic/local when available
everything is easily jazzed up with meat or dairy if that is your thing!
serve the salad below with any of the four slow-cooker recipes, maybe with some bread (wheat, pita, challah or gluten-free) or organic corn chips and hummus

Sweet Salad (for all seasons)

3-4 medium sized apples
8 ounces of raisins
4 ounces of maple syrup
1 medium sized orange
1 teaspoon of apple cider vinegar
3-4 dashes of cinnamon, or to taste
8 ounces of almonds
16 ounces/container of salad greens

Chop apples into tiny little pieces and place them in a bowl. Add raisins, maple syrup, apple cider vinegar, cinnamon. Cut in half and de-seed the orange, then squeeze out the juice on top of everything in the bowl. We like to include the pulp too for flavor/texture. Mix everything very well, cover, and chill for awhile if possible.

Put almonds into food processor and grind them down to powder.

When ready to serve, mix salad greens into the apples+. Once everything is well mixed and all salad greens are wet, pour almonds onto the top of the salad, add one dash of cinnamon on top, and serve.

* sometimes we add a can or two or drained and rinsed chickpeas to the salad for an extra protein kick, especially with the gazpacho below

Watermelon Gazpacho (summer)

I seedless watermelon
4 large tomatoes
I large cucumber, English or otherwise
I/2 large red large onion
handful/sprigs of either dill or mint — to taste
I serrano pepper
4 teaspoons of red wine vinegar

Chop everything only as much as you need to to get items to fit into a blender. Liquify everything and mix all together in a large serving pot. Stir well, chill, and enjoy.

African Stew (autumn)

Dice these vegetables:

1 green bell pepper
1 eggplant, skinned
1 small sweet onion
2 medium zucchinis
1 large carrot
1-2 cloves of garlic, to taste
3 small sweet potatoes, steam them until they soften to reduce slow-cooker time

Put everything in a slow-cooker and then add:

1-2 cups of water
2 cans of chickpeas, drained and rinsed
1 25-ounce jar of pasta sauce
8 ounces of raisins
1/2 teaspoon of ground cinnamon, or more to taste
1/2 teaspoon of cumin, or more to taste
1/2 teaspoon of ground tumeric, or more to taste
1/2 teaspoon of chili powder, or more to taste
a few dashes of ground ginger
salt and pepper to taste

once it starts boiling/bubbling in the crockpot (about 2-3 hours on low) or about an hour before serving, crush some of the sweet potatoes into the broth to thicken (I use a wooden spoon right in the crockpot) and then add a half a bunch of raw kale — or less or more as you like — rinsed, chopped or torn

Sweet Potato Soup/Curried Sweet Potatoes (winter)

chop into approximately one-inch cubes and steam 5-7 large fresh sweet potatoes until very tender and then place them in a large crockpot with . . .

2 cans of coconut milk
about 16 fluid ounces of vegetable broth
about 3-4 fluid ounces of maple syrup
2 cans of cannelini beans, drained and rinsed
many dashes of cinnamon
half as many dashes of ginger
a few dashes of cumin
a few dashes of coriander
*sorry about the spice ratios . . . cooking like Grandma :)
*you can also try it with just cinnamon and it's delicious if you're looking to simplify

once it starts boiling/bubbling in the crockpot (about 2-3 hours on low) or about an hour before serving, crush some of the sweet potatoes into the broth to thicken (I use a wooden spoon right in the crockpot) and then add a half a bunch of raw kale — or less or more as you like — rinsed, chopped or torn

Vegetti (spring)

Super easy! Choose five or so vegetables and cut them up and pour your favorite pasta sauce over them. Here's what I do:

dice these vegetables:

1 green bell pepper
1 eggplant, skinned
1 small sweet onion
2 small yellow squashes
3 small sweet potatoes, steam them until they soften to reduce slow-cooker time

Put everything in a slow-cooker and then add:

half-cup of water
2 cans of cannelini beans, drained and rinsed
2 25-ounce jars of pasta sauce

Mix everything thoroughly in the slow-cooker and cook for 3-4 hours on low. In the last hour, add some rinsed kale, ripped or cut into small pieces. Enjoy!

NOTES

Inspiration & Dedication

My freshman classes read Jesuit Joseph N. Tylenda's *A Pilgrim's Journey: The Autobiography of Ignatius of Loyola* (San Francisco: Ignatius Press, 2001). It is a very accessible translation. I advised my students to skip the two sets of commentary-notes at the bottom of the pages on their first reading the text to get a better glimpse of Ignatius' lived experience before filling in the blanks on dates and places, etc.

Ronald Modras' *Ignatian Humanism: A Dynamic Spirituality for the 21st Century* (Chicago: Loyola, 2004) has some wonderful reflections on Ignatius and Arrupe. His is the best short biography on Arrupe that I have found. It used to bring us all to tears in class to think of Arrupe down by that Hiroshima river as he heard the agonizing cries of burn victims after the blast — a blast set off by our own American authorities during a time of terrible war — as Arrupe heard them drowning. There was nothing he could do. It was darkness when they heard the cries, night. He and his fellow Jesuits were trying to haul up the hill those who had a chance of surviving, trying to get them to their residence and set up a makeshift hospital. And there was only so much they could do in those hours after the blast. But those cries of people slowly drowning in the river as it rose at nightfall . . . people who had gone down to the river to cool the burns on their bodies from the atomic blast and who had found solace in the mud, the wet earth, but now were dying in it, drowning as the waters rose over them.

I always imagine that it was here at this river-bank in the overwhelming darkness of the day's and night's events that "Men for Others" — Arrupe's most famous speech — was written or written from, from this gut-knowledge that we know we can always be more and be mindful for and with one another. And may it be so!

Through my life, I have been influenced by Jesuit David Fleming's *Draw Me Into Your Friendship: The Spiritual Exercises, A Literary Translation & Contemporary Reading* (St. Louis: The Institute of Jesuit Sources, 1996 & 2009). Fleming's careful working with Ignatius' text is fascinating . . . especially the places where Fleming goes silent in areas where Ignatius has a lot to say that might no longer be helpful. Fleming's rendering of Ignatius' First Principle and Foundation is beautiful.

Some Preliminaries Which Might Be Helpful

Regarding the conversation about listening deeply to our friends' stories and, initially, translating them into a language we can better appreciate . . . there's always that tricky question of which comes first, experience or language. With all due respect to theologians David Tracy and Gordon D. Kaufman (see Kaufman's *An Essay on Theological Method.* Atlanta: Scholars Press, 1990) . . . .

Invitations 3 & 5: Mandalas

I learned something like this mandala exercise when I first began the annotated Exercises with my spiritual director. In sessions and on retreats, she encouraged more of a gut-level reaction on the page than a planned one that is popular in Buddhist circles. I believe she was inspired by workshops with Marianne Hieb and Susanne Fincher.

The meditation of imagining you are standing on your mandala and roaming around, as far as I know, is my own. I created it for the senior Meditation elective I once taught at the high school level. It made for a great experience before seeing what the guts might have to say on the type-written page of the actual first quarter exam after reading the works about people doing amazing things through some inner awareness of their own terrains: Paul Farmer, Greg Mortenson, Dorothy Day, Martin Luther King, etc.

Invitations 4 & 6: Joy

For those who might be wondering where in this new setting the First Principle and Foundation is . . . I am imagining this deep-rootedness in joy to be very similar . . . an approach of finding something inside us, inside our human experience, in which to root down instead of overlaying the First Principle upon our experience. For a beautiful modern-rendering of the First Principle and Foundation, see David L. Fleming, S.J.: *Draw Me into Your Friendship*. I think that his modernized First Principle and all of our experiences of joy could very well be in conversation . . .

Invitation 8: Ignatius' Story of Interruption

Thanks go to Ignatius' himself for offering what we have received as his story . . . though those of us interested in those wild, early years before his wounding at age 26 have had to work hard to imagine it because it clearly has been edited out of the received-text. Maybe it was too embarrassing, maybe stories not fit for a saint — stories we all seem to have in our human closets and basements. May the Exercises invite them to be aired out!

As mentioned earlier, I am familiar with Ignatius's story from:

A Pilgrim's Journey: The Autobiography of Ignatius Loyola. Introduction, translation, and commentary by Joseph N. Tylenda, S.J. San Francisco: Ignatius, 2001.

Ignatian Humanism: A Dynamic Spirituality for the 21st Century. Ronald Modras. Chicago, Loyola, 2004.

For a look into Francis of Assisi's story, I am grateful for being a pilgrim with Gillian Ahlgren who introduced me to *The Francis Trilogy of Thomas Celano.* Edited by Regis Armstrong, OFM Cap., J.A. Wayne Hellman, OFM Conv., and William Short, OFM. (Hyde Park, NY: New City Press, 2004).

Invitation 11: A Story

The story's basis is wrapped around an expansion of Mark 5:21 - 43.

Invitation 12: Conversing with a Wisdom Teacher

The texts that follow are all translated by the author from the Greek using *The UBS Greek New Testament* (Stuttgart, Germany: Deutsche Bibelgesellschaft, 2001).

Regarding the *______ in the story:
See Mark 10: 13 - 16 (translation here is the author's): "And children were coming to him so that he might touch them. And his fellow-learners tried to protect his honor — they warned them [the children]. Seeing this, Jesus got all angry and said to them, 'Let the children come to me — don't try to refuse or prevent them! For ones like these are just like the all-pervading-vibe of God that rules everything. Look, this is the way it is: if you are not able to happily welcome the all-pervading-vibe of God as a child, you can't enter into it.' And he took them into his arms and let his good words fall upon them — even placed his hands around them!"

It's easy to note the gospel-writer's shock in that last line, right? It's important to remember that children were barely considered human in the ancient world ... our modern world has barely given them much more until recently: "Little children should be seen, not heard!" The disciples' pushing away the children was their attempt to preserve the honor and dignity of their teacher ... though he has different feelings about that.

While we might not want to admit it ... *"You want to know what the very reality of God is like? Well, it's like a little boy with diarrhea in a freshly filled pool"* is very similar to the idea of Jesus' parables in the Gospel of Matthew 13: 31 & 13: 33:

"And he put another parable to them, 'The all-pervading-vibe of God is like mustard seed that someone took and scattered/sowed in his/her farmland. [...] The all-pervading-vibe of God is like yeast that a woman took and corrupted the wheat-dough — forty-some pounds of it! — until the whole thing was bubbling and rising.'" (translation mine)

Mustard, while useful for cooking/eating and medicine in the ancient world, grew like a weed on the side of the road. Modern equivalents would be dandelions or chickory, that blue-flowered weed used to strengthen rationed coffee during our World Wars. No farmer in his/her right mind today would plant a field of dandelions that, while the chic restaurants might buy some for their ritzy (read: rustic) salads, the seeds would scatter everywhere until you have dandelions growing all over your farmland — especially in places where you do not want them to grow.

Regarding yeast ... see Bernard Brandon Scott's *Hear Then the Parable: A Commentary on the Parables of Jesus* (Minneapolis: Augsburg Fortress, 1989). Pages 325-326 are a good start ... about the measurement-value of three ancient measures of flour, of Jesus' audience's possible reactions to using yeast at certain times of year, and of the surprise character doing anything with dough — let alone so much of it. Joachim Jeremias' *Rediscovering the Parables of Jesus* (New York: Charles Scribner's Sons, 1966, p. 116) might also be helpful.

Arthur Dewey's *The Word in Time* (New Berlin, WI: Liturgical Publications, 1990) offers some playful understandings of the parables as well.

Invitation 13: The Story Continues ...

Luke 18: 10 - 14 (translation by the author) ... "Two guys go up into the temple to pray, one is a Pharisee and the other is a tax collector. The

Pharisee stood off by himself praying out loud (as was the custom), 'I give thanks to you because I am not like the rest of people . . . greedy people, people with no sense of fairness, people who sleep around, or even like this tax collector! I eat nothing two days out of every week and I pay the expected tenth on EVERYTHING I earn!' And there's the tax collector, standing very far away, not coming (forward), not even lifting his eyes to heaven, but beating his chest and saying, 'O God, be merciful to me with my shortcomings.'

Pharisees were like the lay religious educators of their day who held some — though precarious — power in the Jewish world at this time. While the priests ruled the rituals and the religious-observances, the Pharisees ruled the story and its interpretation. The priests' claim to power was in the Law, the Torah, the 613 laws that confirmed their power. While the Pharisees recognized the authority of the Torah, they also saw importance in the prophets, those iconoclasts that often were at odds with the emerging religious-observance tradition. The prophets often called out people when their hearts were not into it, when ritual was performed only to appease God in order that one may do whatever one wished. Some have summed up the prophets with one simple statement: Turn your heart back to God — repent, feel again! The tax collectors were hated by just about everybody because no one ever really knew how much of the money they collected went to the Roman authorities who employed them and how much of the money they legally pocketed for themselves. No God-respecting Pharisee would allow a tax collector anywhere near the temple — no matter the Pharisee's probable disdain for the priests' power to rule the workings of the temple-space based in the Law. Do you notice how in this ancient story, what one would expect to come out of the Pharisee's mouth comes out of the tax collector's mouth . . . and maybe even vice versa. Such is human nature, and we would be wise and probably honest to find ourselves in both the Pharisee and the tax collector of the story at times in our lives, right? We're all human . . . . and that's the gift!

What's even more interesting to me is the teller of this little parabolic story (Jesus). As we all know, Jesus was Jewish, and while scholars agree Jesus was not a Pharisee (a Jewish leader of the day), the understanding of life that comes forth in Jesus' parables and wisdom-sayings would line up quite a bit with what the Pharisees put forward. Both Jesus and the Pharisees appear to have great respect for the prophets, especially their playfulness in storytelling and in re-imagining their world through clever sayings. For both Jesus and the Pharisees, everything is continually in motion, not much is ever completely decided upon, everything can be looked at and heard and discovered in new ways. That is to say, something new can be born through uttering some clever new words — a story, a saying, a parable that wraps itself around your mind and waits for you to realize a bigger world, that waits for you to let go of the old way of seeing for something a little closer to the infinite reality, the bigger vision. Though they seem to have much to argue about, Jesus and the Pharisees appear to have a lot in common, which leads me to wonder if this parable of the Pharisee and the Tax Collector ("Two guys go up to the temple to pray") could be Jesus gently poking a little fun at his own self, at the ways he and others sometimes get mired in the drying concrete of one way of experiencing life instead of being open to what the moment presents.

In any case, we would do well to avoid the pitfall of arguing that Jesus hates the Pharisees, whose philosophy gives birth to modern, rabbinic Judaism. For a more in-depth study of the Pharisees, see J. Andrew Overman's *Matthew's Gospel and Formative Judaism: The Social World of the Matthean Community*. (Minneapolis: Augsburg Fortress, 1990) and *The Complete Gospels*. Robert J. Miller, editor (Salem, OR: Polebridge, 2010). Overman's book examines the writer(s) of the Gospel of Matthew, Pharisee(s), and the crises that give birth to the Gospel of Matthew where something new is brought forward from something old, the whole process of ancient wisdom.

Matthew 5: 45 (translation by the author) . . . "because he makes the sun rise on the worthless-degenerates and the good-guys and sends rain on the honest and the dishonest . . ."

Invitation 14: Home and Back Again

Matthew 7: 3 (translation by the author) . . . "Why do you see the little speck in your brother's eye but in your own eye there's a log you don't even notice!"

Invitation 15: Considering Forgiveness

Matthew 6: 12 (translation by the author) . . . speaking to God: ". . . and let go/forgive us our debts as just as we let go/forgive the ones in debt to us."

The Knower is a reference to the Bhagavad Gita. Sri Swami Satchidananda's *The Living Gita* (Yogaville/Buckingham, VA: Integral Yoga

Publications, 2012) is a playful translation and commentary of this classic text.

Invitation 16: An Ease . . . A Disruption

Matthew 6: 25 - 30 (translation by the author) . . . " . . . do not worry about your life, what you are eating, what you are drinking, and not about your body — what you are wearing. Isn't your life much more than food and the body much more than clothes? Watch for awhile the birds of the sky, how they don't plant seeds, they don't harvest, they don't gather into barns for storage . . . and yet Someone gives them food . . . aren't you worth more than they are?! How from your worrying can you add one forearm's length to the height and breadth of your life? And why worry about your clothes? Learn something from the flowers of the field — how do they grow? They don't struggle or work hard or spin thread for clothes. And I say to you that not even the famously rich and beautiful King Solomon in all his radiant-beauty was clothed like one of these! If Someone dresses up the field-grass in this way — field-grass which lives today and tomorrow is thrown into the burning-oven — aren't you better than them, you who trust so little?"

Luke 6: 20b (translation by the author) . . . "Congratulations, you beggars, you poor! The Universe, the very reality of God belongs to you!"

Invitation 17: Take Nothing with You for the Journey!

"Take nothing with you for the journey . . ." references Mark 6: 7 - 13, and then also Luke 9: 1 - 6 & Matthew 10: 5 - 15.

"Ask for what you really, really need . . ." references Matthew 7: 7 - 8.

"After all, all of the greats were wanderers as well, so no need to feel so tied down here to this particular place" references Deuteronomy 26: 5 and soooo many references to great ones like Gandhi and Dr. Martin Luther King, Jr. who allowed even something as uncomfortable as a jail cell to be their place of prayer and meditation, their home.

"Just get moving" references Gospel of Thomas 42, so nicely translated and understood by Robert W. Funk, Arthur J. Dewey, and the Jesus Seminar in *The Gospel of Jesus* (Salem, OR: Polebridge, 2015).

"Birds have nests . . ." references Matthew 8: 20

Invitation 18: In Your Home

"Hey, what you pile up in your treasure-chest is there in your heart too, you know?" is a translation by the author of Matthew 6: 21.

"I love my lovers! My seekers find me!
Rich and distinguished are they who are with me!
What's valuable grows ... honesty ... the truest of intentions!
My fruit is better than gold — the finest gold!" is a translation from the Hebrew by the author of Proverbs 8: 17 - 19a from the Hebrew text *Biblia Hebraica Stuttgartensia* (Stuttgart, Germany: Deutsche Bibelgesellschaft, 1990).

The remaining references to Wisdom being older than the hills, building a house, throwing a banquet are paraphrases of Proverbs 9: 1 - 11.

Sophia, of course, has been known through the centuries as the feminine embodiment of Wisdom. It's a name and understanding nearly older than the hills ....

Invitation 19: Dancing with Sophia?

There are some lovely movement concepts in the Feldenkrais tradition of Awareness Through Movement . . . especially in the work of Ruthy Alon through Movement Intelligence (Bones for Life). Check to see if there are practitioners in your area that might be able to share some of the practice with you through classes or private sessions. The movement is so gentle and nice, restores innocence to ourselves.

And there are some wonderful things to consider in unscripted/reactive yoga and dance that are being re-discovered again. Indeed, just what was the dance of David (II Samuel 6) but an inspired movement in reaction to the moment ... a movement fit even for a nearly-naked king? Perhaps we would be so wise to flow like the ocean and gently move as we feel called to gently move from within our deepest selves?

Invitation 22: Once You Have Your List Ready ...

Matthew 5:44 (translation by the author) ..."Love your hated-enemies with all you have/are, and pray for the ones who press down upon you and run after you and persecute you."

I am incredibly grateful to Arthur Dewey for first leading me to consider the depth of this saying and for turning me on to Walter Wink's inspiring and challenging *Engaging the Powers: Discernment and Resistance in a World of Domination* (Minneapolis: Augsburg Fortress, 1992) and much of Wink's other work, including *Jesus and Nonviolence: A Third Way.*

Invitation 23: A Meditation

Author's version of a Buddhist Tonglen practice, though one can find such gentle-surrender in Islam, Sufism, perhaps in all traditions.

Invitation 24: An Old Way Brought Forward Again and Again and Again . . . for a New Future in this Profound Present

Matthew 5: 38-41 (translation by the author) . . . "Do not set yourself up against someone intending to hold power over you. Instead, whoever slaps you on your right cheek, turn to him the other! And as for the one about to sue you to take even your underwear, offer to him your jacket as well! And if someone forces you into service for one thousand paces, go with him two thousand paces!"

Again, see Walter Wink's wonderfully accessible look into these sayings' possibilities in *Engaging the Powers: Discernment and Resistance in a World of Domination.* (Minneapolis: Augsburg Fortress, 1992).

Invitation 25: Reflecting on Nonviolence . . . Jujitsu

For an inspiring look into Gandhi's life, there is of course the incredible movie *Gandhi* (1982, directed by Richard Attenborough). I have been grateful for *The Essential Gandhi: An Anthology of His Writings on His Life, Work and Ideas.* Mahatma Gandhi. Edited by Louis Fischer. (New York: Vintage, 1962). See especially pp 170, 315.

For one of the best books I have read on Rosa Parks' courage and on/by Dr. Martin Luther King, Jr., see *Stride Toward Freedom: The Montgomery Story* (New York: HarperCollins, 1958). Meet King before he's on the international stage . . . a most moving and inspiring account of the beginnings of the Civil Rights Movement.

Invitation 26: Practice a Day of Mindful Ease

"Walking . . . what is now being considered the best medicine for the whole body" from this invitation references the incredibly inspiring book by Norman Doidge, M.D., *The Brain's Way of Healing: Remarkable Discoveries and*

Recoveries from the Frontiers of Neuroplasticity (New York: Viking, 2015). See especially page p. 85.

Invitation 28: Looking Through You . . .

Though I think I have always been in the habit of writing with both hands for different reasons, I have learned much by consulting *The Power of Your Other Hand: A Course in Channeling the Inner Wisdom of the Right Brain* by Lucia Capacchione, Ph.D. (Franklin Lakes, NJ: New Page Books, 2001).

Invitations 36 - 40 . . . on lament

Dr. Walter Brueggemann, perhaps the greatest imaginer of the Hebrew Scriptures of our day, inspired these sections on lament that appear in these "Week Three" invitations. Dr. Brueggemann's Lenten lecture series at Episcopal Church of the Redeemer and around Greater Cincinnati in 2010 and 2011 have given many of us reason to imagine new ways of proceeding in our culture and our grief-filled lives around the world. I too have been greatly aided by his groundbreaking book *The Prophetic Imagination* (Minneapolis?: Fortess Press, 1978) in just about every way I imagine the scriptures and storytelling. We are grateful that Dr. Brueggemann has given permission to us to share and expand upon some of his ideas on lament in this new setting. It should go without saying, though, that any errors in this author's understandings of lament are the author's errors and not Dr. Brueggemann's.

Invitation 37: Ancient Lament . . . our ancestors' way of praying

Translation of Psalm 44 is by the author using the Hebrew text referenced earlier in Invitation 18's notes.

Invitation 41: From Where Do the Words Come?

For more information on this tragedy: http://www.cnn.com/2007/US/04/18/vtech.shooting/index.html

Invitations 43, 45, 47, and 49 . . . on pregnancy

Many of us at VITALITY have been inspired by the work of English/Drama-teacher-turned-Jungian-analyst Marion Woodman:

The Pregnant Virgin: A Process of Psychological Transformation (Toronto: Inner City, 1985)

Addiction to Perfection: The Still Unravished Bride (Toronto: Inner City, 1982)

Leaving My Father's House: A Journey to Conscious Femininity, with Kate Danson, Mary Hamilton, Rita Greer Alen (Boston: Shambhala, 1993)

Dancing in the Flames: The Dark Goddess in the Transformation of Consciousness, with Elinor Dickson (Boston: Shambhala, 1997)

For further exploration . . . we invite you to check out these works which continue to inspire us to look within and trust:

Sabbath: Finding Rest, Renewal, and Delight in Our Busy Lives. Wayne Muller. New York: Bantam, 1999.

I Will Not Die an Unlived Life: Reclaiming Purpose and Passion. Dawna Markova. San Francisco: Donari, 2000.

The Artist's Way: A Spiritual Path to Higher Creativity. Julia Cameron. New York: Putnam, 1992.

ABOUT THE AUTHORS

VITALITY Cincinnati was founded in 2010 when friends taking Healing Touch Level 4 connected with a common desire to make holistic self-care education affordable and accessible in Cincinnati. Many friends joined us as we imagined together a new way of living personally and communally, We began by offering free/donation-based Healing Touch sessions around Cincinnati: on college campuses, at social service agencies and food pantries, at health fairs and conferences. We became a 501(c)3 non-profit organization on December 3 of that first year together - Francis Xavier's feast day.

In January 2011, with the help of many friends, we renovated a storefront in the heart of the city (Norwood) on Montgomery Rd. - on a major bus-line, with plenty of walk-by traffic and plenty of on-street and free parking, in walking distance to Xavier University. We offered Healing Touch sessions, yoga classes for many levels of practice, meditation opportunities, Inner Journaling meditation-journaling-conversation groups, and our first Healing Touch Level I class . . . all in exchange for a cash donation or community service. All participants were invited to share their gifts to grow the health and vitality of our city.

In Fall 2011, we offered our first Yoga/Healing Touch Internship. Participants paid $100 to receive their 200-hour yoga teacher's certification and two levels of Healing Touch classes . . . and were asked to give-back over 100 hours of free/donation-based yoga classes, Healing Touch sessions, and meditation opportunities at VITALITY and throughout our city. Five people graduated from our first internship. Two completed the program in our second year. When we hired a Program Director to expand the internship, twenty graduated our third year, and seventeen our fourth year.

In January 2015, we re-focused our Yoga/Healing Touch Internship to be more neighborhood-based. Walnut Hills, the first neighborhood of Cincinnati, was our first neighborhood. Twelve neighbors gathered on Saturdays to train through our Yoga/Healing Touch Internship offered at the Walnut Hills Redevelopment Foundation offices, worked at our Wednesday night free classes at the Dr. Dillard Center in the heart of Walnut Hlls, and offered 100 hours of service in the Walnut Hills community gardens. Three vacant lots that had become problematic over the years now thrive as parks and dedicated community gardens. One garden, an overgrown lot full of weeds, now boasts fifty large beds with rich soil, a retention pond made out of old tires from the neighborhood, a tool shed made out of old doors from the neighborhood, a green house made with old windows and a solar panel . . . and a community that now meets there to grow food for themselves and their families and friends. The twelve Yoga/Healing Touch graduates of the program now continue those Wednesday night yoga classes and have expanded to a few more days a week. Residents and friends of Walnut HIlls continue to enjoy yoga/wellness opportunities thanks to these new yoga teachers who keep the donations from their classes to grow their families and lives.

This Fall 2015, we our working with Avondale, a neighbor to Walnut Hills. Our hope is to work with a new community each Spring and Fall so that yoga/wellness teachers can be trained and then create together whatever they envision is important for their community.

In 2015, we added Bones for Life/Movement Intelligence -- the incredible work by Feldenkrais trainer Ruthy Alon -- to our offerings in addition to our Spiritual Exercises storytelling groups. A 300-hour capstone yoga certification is on the horizon as well. Every one of our offerings invites participants to explore their own resourcefulness through self-care.

Purchase of *A New Setting of Ignatius' Spiritual Exercises* supports the work of VITALITY Cincinnati, which shares holistic self-care education neighborhood by neighborhood, person to person, and breath by breath through Greater Cincinnati. With an annual budget of $60,000, we are able to invite amazing things, many opportunities for embodiment, for knowing the heart of life, for letting ourselves begin to slow down and listen for that inner teacher inviting us to life and to life and to life, no matter the journey before us. We are friends, imperfect people growing in authenticity every day. We are grateful for your participation!

Publication of this book has been underwritten by Peg & Joe Conway, in gratitude for the healing mission of VITALITY Cincinnati. We are grateful to you, Conway Family!

Please visit our website: vitalitycincinnati.org

CPSIA information can be obtained
at www.ICGtesting.com
Printed in the USA
FFOW05n1255121015

9 781457 541537